MW00341904

28 Terrific quilts that are simp

Best of Fons&Porter
Easy Collection

LEISURE ARTS®
the art of everyday living
www.leisurearts.com

FONS & PORTER STAFF
Editors-in-Chief Marianne Fons and Liz Porter

Editor Jean Nolte
Associate Editor Diane Tomlinson
Managing Editor Debra Finan
Technical Writer Kristine Peterson

Art Director Tony Jacobson

Interactive Editor Morgan Abel
Sewing Specialist Colleen Tauke
Contributing Photographers Dean Tanner, Katie Downey, Craig Anderson
Contributing Photo Assistant DeElda Wittmack

Publisher Kristi Loeffelholz
Advertising Manager Cristy Adamski
Retail Manager Sharon Hart
Web Site Manager Phillip Zacharias
Fons & Porter Staff Shelle Goodwin, Sheyenne Manning, Anne Welker, Karla Wesselmann, Kelsey Wolfswinkel

New Track Media LLC
President and CEO Stephen J. Kent
Chief Financial Officer Mark F. Arnett
President, Book Publishing W. Budge Wallis
Vice President/Group Publisher Tina Battock
Vice President, Consumer Marketing, CMO Nicole McGuire
Vice President, Production Barbara Schmitz
Production Manager Dominic M. Taormina
Production Coordinator Jennifer Creasey
IT Manager Denise Donnarumma

Our Mission Statement
Our goal is for you to enjoy making quilts as much as we do.

EDITORIAL STAFF
Vice President of Editorial: Susan White Sullivan
Creative Art Director: Katherine Laughlin
Publications Director: Leah Lampirez
Special Projects Director: Susan Frantz Wiles
Prepress Technician: Stephanie Johnson

BUSINESS STAFF
President and Chief Executive Officer: Rick Barton
Senior Vice President of Operations: Jim Dittrich
Vice President of Finance: Fred F. Pruss
Vice President of Sales-Retail Books: Martha Adams
Vice President of Mass Market: Bob Bewighouse
Vice President of Technology and Planning: Laticia Mull Dittrich
Controller: Tiffany P. Childers
Information Technology Director: Brian Roden
Director of E-Commerce: Mark Hawkins
Manager of E-Commerce: Robert Young
Retail Customer Service Manager: Stan Raynor

Library of Congress Control Number:2013957627
ISBN-13/EAN: 978-1-4647-0873-2
UPC: 0-28906-06053-9

10 9 8 7 6 5 4 3 2 1

We hope you'll enjoy this collection of easy quilt patterns. Each can be made in a weekend or less. Simplified patchwork, larger blocks, strip sets, and other shortcuts make it all possible without sacrificing beauty. While these quilts are a perfect choice for beginning quilters, they are also great for more experienced quilters who are looking for projects they can finish quickly. As you browse through the pages, we think you'll find plenty of inspiration for your next quilt.

Happy quilting,

Marianne & Liz

Table of Contents

96

54

64

Jake's Escalator

This easy quilt is actually one gigantic Jacob's Ladder block.
The fun zigzag border is made with triangle-squares.

PROJECT RATING: EASY

Size: 80" × 80"

MATERIALS

⅝ yard large floral
1 yard small floral
1½ yards navy stripe
2⅛ yards navy print
1 fat quarter★ navy-and-green print
1⅜ yards aqua print
¾ yard blue print
1 yard green print
Fons & Porter Half & Quarter
    Ruler (optional)
7½ yards backing fabric
Queen-size quilt batting
★fat quarter = 18" × 20"

Cutting

Measurements include ¼" seam
allowances. Instructions are written for
using the Fons & Porter Half & Quarter
Ruler. If not using this ruler, follow
cutting NOTES.

From large floral, cut:

- 2 (8½"-wide) strips. From strips, cut 6 (8½") D squares.

From small floral, cut:

- 1 (8½"-wide) strip. From strip, cut 4 (8½") D squares.
- 5 (4½"-wide) strips. From strips, cut 68 half-square B triangles.
  NOTE: If not using the Fons & Porter Half & Quarter Ruler, cut 5 (4⅞"-wide) strips. From strips, cut 34 (4⅞") squares. Cut squares in half diagonally to make 68 half-square B triangles.

From navy stripe, cut:

- 6 (8½"-wide) strips. From strips, cut 24 (8½") D squares.

From navy print, cut:

- 2 (8⅞"-wide) strips. From strips, cut 5 (8⅞") squares. Cut squares in half diagonally to make 10 half-square A triangles.
- 4 (8½"-wide) strips. From strips, cut 16 (8½") D squares.
- 9 (2¼"-wide) strips for binding.

From navy-and-green print fat quarter, cut:

- 2 (8½"-wide) strips. From strips, cut 4 (8½") D squares.

From aqua print, cut:

- 2 (8⅞"-wide) strips. From strips, cut 5 (8⅞") squares. Cut squares in half diagonally to make 10 half-square A triangles.
- 6 (4½"-wide) strips. From strips, cut 76 half-square B triangles.
  NOTE: If not using the Fons & Porter Half & Quarter Ruler, cut 5 (4⅞"-wide) strips. From strips, cut 38 (4⅞") squares. Cut squares in half diagonally to make 76 half-square B triangles.

From blue print, cut:

- 5 (4½"-wide) strips. From strips, cut 64 half-square B triangles.
  NOTE: If not using the Fons & Porter Half & Quarter Ruler, cut 4 (4⅞"-wide) strips. From strips, cut 32 (4⅞") squares. Cut squares in half diagonally to make 64 half-square B triangles.

From green print, cut:

- 6 (4½"-wide) strips. From strips, cut 4 (4½") C squares and 72 half-square B triangles.

  NOTE: If not using the Fons & Porter Half & Quarter Ruler, cut 5 (4⅞"-wide) strips. From strips, cut 36 (4⅞") squares. Cut squares in half diagonally to make 72 half-square B triangles.

Block Assembly

1. Join 1 navy print A triangle and 1 aqua print A triangle as shown in *Triangle-Square Diagrams*. Make 10 large triangle-squares.

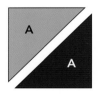

Triangle-Square Diagrams

2. In the same manner, join 1 small floral B triangle and 1 aqua print B triangle to make 1 small triangle-square. Make 36 small floral/aqua print small triangle-squares. Make 32 small triangle-squares using small floral and blue print B triangles, 40 small triangle-squares using green print and aqua print B triangles, and 32 small triangle-squares using green print and blue print B triangles.

Border Assembly

1. Lay out 2 green/aqua small triangle-squares, 1 small floral/blue small triangle-square, and 1 small floral/aqua small triangle-square as shown in *Border Unit 1 Diagrams*. Join into rows; join rows to complete 1 Border Unit 1. Make 16 Border Unit 1.

Border Unit 1 Diagrams

2. In the same manner, lay out 2 green/blue small triangle squares, 1 small floral/blue small triangle-square, and 1 small floral/aqua small triangle-square. Join into rows; join rows to complete 1 Border Unit 2 *(Border Unit 2 Diagram)*. Make 16 Border Unit 2.

Border Unit 2 Diagram

3. Lay out 4 Border Unit 1 and 4 Border Unit 2 as shown in *Quilt Top Assembly Diagram*. Join to make 1 border. Make 4 borders.

4. Lay out 1 small floral/aqua small triangle-square, 2 green/aqua small triangle-squares, and 1 green print C square as shown in *Corner Unit Diagrams*. Join into rows; join rows. Make 4 Corner Units.

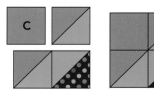

Corner Unit Diagrams

Quilt Assembly

1. Lay out large triangle-squares and D squares as shown in *Quilt Top Assembly Diagram*. Join into rows; join rows to complete quilt center.

2. Add 1 border to each side of quilt center.

3. Add 1 Corner Unit to each end of remaining borders. Add borders to top and bottom of quilt.

Finishing

1. Divide backing into 3 (2½-yard) lengths. Join panels lengthwise.

2. Layer backing, batting, and quilt top; baste. Quilt as desired. Quilt shown was quilted with an allover design of flowers and feathers *(Quilting Diagram)*.

3. Join 2¼"-wide navy print strips into 1 continuous piece for straight-grain French-fold binding. Add binding to quilt.

Quilting Diagram

DESIGNER

Yolanda Fundora is a fabric and pattern designer and quilt book author. She calls her quilt and fabric design business UrbanAmish™, and teaches her concepts on her blog.

Quilt Top Assembly Diagram

Mod Garden

Make this easy quilt using a traditional block and a collection of cheery fabrics.
It's sure to bring a smile to your face.

PROJECT RATING: EASY

Size: 63" × 80½"

Blocks:

18 (8¾") Irish Chain blocks

MATERIALS

3½ yards white print for blocks
   and border
1½ yards yellow print for blocks,
   yo-yos, and binding
1 yard light teal print for blocks
⅜ yard dark teal print
1 yard light coral print for blocks
⅜ yard dark coral print
1¾ yards moss print for border
Paper-backed fusible web
4 yards backing fabric
Full-size quilt batting

Cutting

Measurements include ¼" seam allowances. Border strips are exact length needed. You may want to make them longer to allow for piecing variations. Patterns for appliqué shapes and yo-yo circle are on page 14. Follow manufacturer's instructions for using fusible web.

From white print, cut:

- 7 (8½"-wide) strips. Piece strips to make 2 (8½" × 65") side outer borders and 2 (8½" × 63½") top and bottom outer borders.
- 7 (5¾"-wide) strips. From 5 strips, cut 17 (5¾" ×9¼") A rectangles. Remaining strips are for strip sets.
- 4 (2¼"-wide) strips for strip sets.
- 6 (1⅛"-wide) strips. Piece strips to make 2 (1⅛" × 61¾") side inner borders and 2 (1⅛" × 45½") top and bottom inner borders.

From yellow print, cut:

- 17 (2¼"-wide) strips for strip sets and binding.
- 18 Yo-yo Circles.

From light teal print, cut:

- 8 (2¼"-wide) strips for strip sets.
- 9 Small Circles.

From dark teal print, cut:

- 9 Large Circles.

From light coral print, cut:

- 8 (2¼"-wide) strips for strip sets.
- 9 Small Circles.

From dark coral print, cut:

- 9 Large Circles.

From moss print, cut:

- 6 (1½"-wide) strips. Piece strips to make 2 (1½" × 63") side middle borders and 2 (1½" × 47½") top and bottom middle borders.
- 420" of (2"-wide) **bias** strips. Join strips. Fold strips in thirds; press and hand baste folds in place to prepare vines for appliqué.
- 47 Leaves.

Irish Chain Block Assembly

1. Join 2 yellow print strips, 2 light coral print strips, and 1 white print (2¼"-wide) strip as shown in *Strip Set #1 Diagram*. Make 2 Strip Set #1. From strip sets, cut 36 (2¼"-wide) #1 segments.

> ### Sew **Smart**™
> When joining strips for strip sets, alternate sewing direction from strip to strip. This keeps strip sets straight.—Marianne

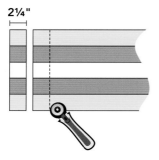

Strip Set #1 Diagram

2. Join 2 light teal print strips, 2 yellow print strips, and 1 light coral print strip as shown in *Strip Set #2 Diagram*. Make 2 Strip Set #2. From strip sets, cut 36 (2¼"-wide) #2 segments.

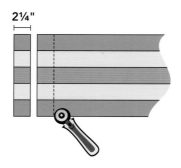

Strip Set #2 Diagram

3. Join 2 white print (2¼"-wide) strips, 2 light teal print strips, and 1 yellow print strip as shown in *Strip Set #3 Diagram*. From strip set, cut 18 (2¼"-wide) #3 segments.

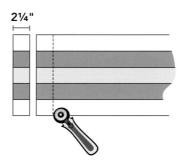

Strip Set #3 Diagram

4. Lay out 2 #1 segments, 2 #2 segments, and 1 #3 segment as shown in *Irish Chain Block Assembly Diagram*. Join segments to complete 1 Irish Chain block *(Irish Chain Block Diagram)*. Make 18 Irish Chain blocks.

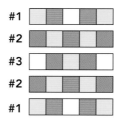

Irish Chain Block Assembly Diagram

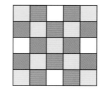

Irish Chain Block Diagram

Setting Block Assembly

1. Join 2 light coral print strips and 1 white print (5¾"-wide) strip as shown in *Strip Set #4 Diagram*. From strip set, cut 16 (2¼"-wide) coral #4 segments.

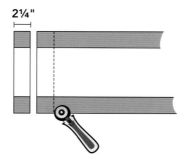

Strip Set #4 Diagram

2. Join 2 light teal print strips and 1 white print (5¾"-wide) strip as shown in *Strip Set #5 Diagram*. From strip set, cut 18 (2¼"-wide) teal #4 segments.

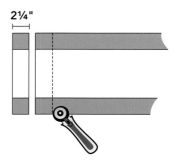

Strip Set #5 Diagram

3. Lay out 2 #4 segments and 1 white print A rectangle as shown in *Setting Block Assembly Diagram*. Join to complete 1 setting block *(Setting Block Diagrams)*. Make 8 coral setting blocks and 9 teal setting blocks.

Setting Block Assembly Diagram

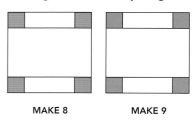

MAKE 8   MAKE 9

Setting Block Diagram

Quilt Assembly

1. Lay out blocks as shown in *Quilt Top Assembly Diagram*.

2. Join blocks into rows; join rows to complete quilt center.

3. Add white print side inner borders to quilt center. Add white print top and bottom inner borders to quilt.

4. Repeat for moss print middle borders and white print outer borders.

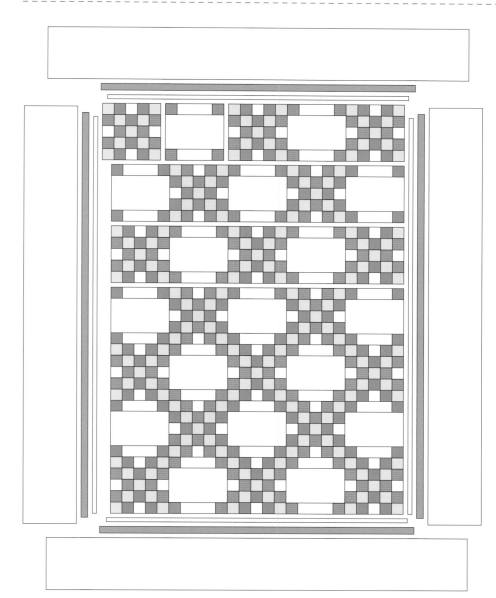

Quilt Top Assembly Diagram

3. Join 2¼"-wide yellow print strips into 1 continuous piece for straight-grain French-fold binding. Add binding to quilt.

Quilting Diagram

DESIGNER

Patti Carey loves to design quilts, and hopes to inspire other quilters with her creations. ✳

Appliqué Border

1. Referring to quilt photo on page 11, arrange vine, leaves, coral circles, and teal circles on outer border; fuse in place. Appliqué using matching thread.

> ### Sew **Smart**™
> Go to FonsandPorter.com/windowfuse to learn how to reduce bulk in fusible appliqué.
> —Marianne

2. Referring to *Sew Easy: Making Yo-Yos* on page 15, make 18 yellow yo-yos.

3. Appliqué yo-yos to large circles.

Finishing

1. Divide backing into 2 (2-yard) lengths. Join panels lengthwise. Seam will run horizontally.

2. Layer backing, batting, and quilt top; baste. Quilt as desired. Quilt shown was quilted with a flower design in quilt center and continuous loops and curves in appliqué border *(Quilting Diagram).*

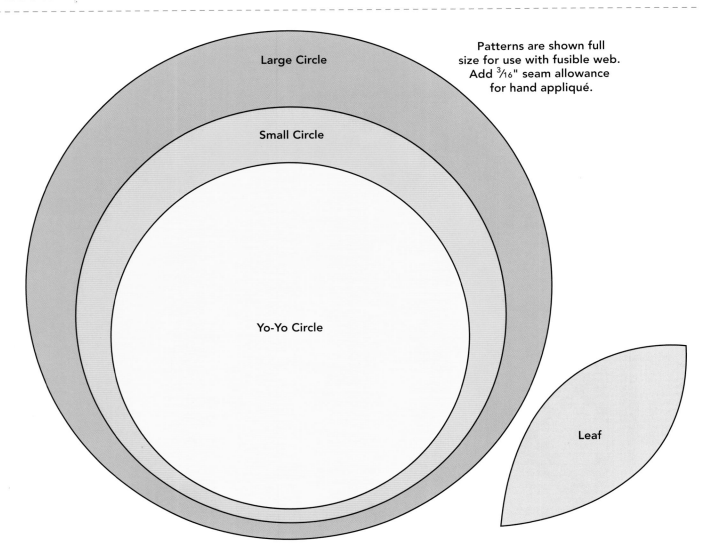

Large Circle

Small Circle

Yo-Yo Circle

Leaf

Patterns are shown full size for use with fusible web. Add ³/₁₆" seam allowance for hand appliqué.

SIZE OPTIONS

	Crib (45½" × 45½")	Queen (98" × 98")
Setting	3 × 3	9 × 9

MATERIALS

White Print	2 yards	7 yards
Yellow Print	¾ yard	2½ yards
Light Teal Print	½ yard	2 yards
Dark Teal Print	1 fat quarter★	⅝ yard
Light Coral Print	½ yard	2 yards
Dark Coral Print	1 fat quarter★	⅝ yard
Moss Print	1 yard	2¾ yards
Backing Fabric	2¾ yards	9 yards
Batting	Crib-Size	King-Size

★fat quarter = 18" × 20"

Web **Extra**

Go to FonsandPorter.com/modgardensizes to download *Quilt Top Assembly Diagrams* for these size options.

Making Yo-Yos

Follow these simple steps to make yo-yos for *Mod Garden* on page 10.

1. Cut circle using Yo-Yo Circle pattern.
2. Turn under raw edge of cirlce ¼" to wrong side and take small running stitches around edge through both layers *(Photo A)*. Use quilting thread or other strong thread that will not break when gathering.
3. Pull thread to gather circle with right side of fabric facing out. Make a knot to hold circle closed. Gathered side is front of yo-yo *(Photo B)*.

> ## Sew **Smart**™
> Do not make running stitches too small. Longer stitches make the circle easier to gather, and the "hole" smaller.
> — Marianne

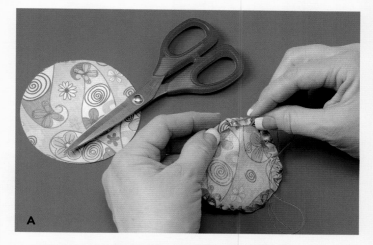

A

B

Aromatherapy

This quilt has just twenty-four easy-to-piece blocks arranged in a simple setting. Beginners and experienced quilters alike will enjoy how quickly it goes together.

PROJECT RATING: EASY

Size: 49" × 69"

Blocks: 24 (8") Half Log Cabin blocks

MATERIALS

1 fat quarter★ green print for blocks

1 yard gray print for blocks and binding

¾ yard multicolor print for blocks

¾ yard white print for blocks

⅞ yard teal print for sashing

1 fat quarter★ white solid for sashing squares

1⅛ yards white large floral for border

3 yards backing fabric

Twin-size quilt batting

★fat quarter = 18" × 20"

Cutting

Measurements include ¼" seam allowances. Border strips are exact length needed. You may want to cut them longer to allow for piecing variations.

From green print fat quarter, cut:

• 3 (4½"-wide) strips. From strips, cut 12 (4½") A squares.

From gray print, cut:

• 2 (4½"-wide) strips. From strips, cut 12 (4½") A squares.

• 7 (2¼"-wide) strips for binding.

From multicolor print, cut:

• 9 (2½"-wide) strips. From strips, cut 12 (2½" × 8½") D rectangles, 24 (2½" × 6½") C rectangles, and 12 (2½" × 4½") B rectangles.

From white print, cut:

• 9 (2½"-wide) strips. From strips, cut 12 (2½" × 8½") D rectangles, 24 (2½" × 6½") C rectangles, and 12 (2½" × 4½") B rectangles.

From teal print, cut:

• 10 (2½"-wide) strips. From strips, cut 38 (2½" × 8½") D rectangles.

From white solid fat quarter, cut:

• 3 (2½"-wide) strips. From strips, cut 15 (2½") E squares.

From white large floral, cut:

• 6 (6"-wide) strips. Piece strips to make 2 (6" × 58½") side borders and 2 (6" × 49½") top and bottom borders.

Block Assembly

1. Lay out 1 gray print A square, 1 each multicolor print B and C rectangles, and 1 each white print C and D rectangles as shown in *Block Assembly Diagram.*

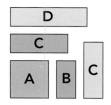

Block Assembly Diagram

2. Join to complete 1 Block *(Block Diagrams)*. Make 12 gray blocks.

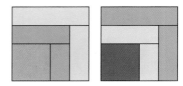

Make 12   **Make 12**

Block Diagrams

3. In the same manner, make 12 green blocks, using 1 green print A square, 1 each white print B and C rectangles, and 1 each multicolor print C and D rectangles.

Quilt Assembly

1. Lay out blocks, teal print D rectangles, and white solid E squares as shown in *Quilt Top Assembly Diagram*. Join into rows; join rows to complete quilt center.

2. Add white large floral side borders to quilt center. Add top and bottom borders to quilt.

Finishing

1. Divide backing into 2 (1½-yard) lengths. Join panels lengthwise. Seam will run horizontally.

2. Layer backing, batting, and quilt top; baste. Quilt as desired. Quilt shown was quilted with an allover large floral design *(Quilting Diagram)*.

3. Join 2¼"-wide gray print strips into 1 continuous piece for straight-grain French-fold binding. Add binding to quilt.

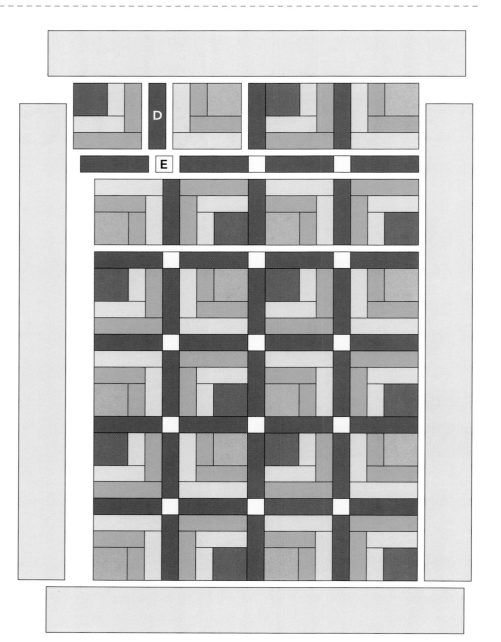

Quilt Top Assembly Diagram

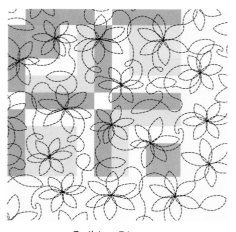

Quilting Diagram

SIZE OPTIONS

	Twin (69" × 89")	Full (79" × 89")	Queen (89" × 99")
Blocks	48	56	72
Setting	6 × 8	7 × 8	8 × 9

MATERIALS

	Twin (69" × 89")	Full (79" × 89")	Queen (89" × 99")
Green Print	½ yard	⅝ yard	¾ yard
Gray Print	1 yard	1¼ yards	1⅜ yards
Multicolor Print	1¼ yards	1⅝ yards	2 yards
White Print	1¼ yards	1⅝ yards	2 yards
Teal Print	1⅝ yards	1⅞ yards	2⅜ yards
White Solid	¼ yard	¼ yard	⅜ yard
White Large Floral	1⅜ yards	1⅝ yards	2 yards
Backing Fabric	5½ yards	5½ yards	8¼ yards
Batting	Twin-size	Full-size	Queen-size

Web **Extra**

Go to FonsandPorter.com/jaaroma to download *Quilt Top Assembly Diagrams* for these size options.

TRIED & TRUE

We featured a fun seasonal print and coordinates in our block. The fabric collection is Haunted Hollow II, Bats, Hats and Alley Cats by Jacqueline Paton for Red Rooster Fabrics.

Snapshot

This quilt goes together very quickly.
You can easily piece it in a weekend—or at your next quilt retreat.

PROJECT RATING: EASY

Size: 70" × 84"

Blocks: 30 (14") blocks

MATERIALS

⅜ yard each of 15 assorted prints in
   yellow, red, gray, and turquoise

1⅝ yards gray print for sashing

1½ yards black print for blocks and
   binding

5 yards backing fabric

Twin-size quilt batting

Cutting

Measurements include ¼" seam
allowances.

From each ⅜ yard piece, cut:

- 1 (6½"-wide) strip. From strip, cut 4
  (6½") A squares and 4 (3½") B squares.
- 2 (2½"-wide) strips. From strips, cut
  4 (2½" × 6½") F rectangles and 4
  (2½"× 4½") E rectangles.

From gray print, cut:

- 8 (6½"-wide) strips. From strips, cut
  120 (6½" × 2½") F rectangles.

From black print, cut:

- 2 (2½"-wide) strips. From strips, cut
  30 (2½") G squares.
- 9 (2¼"-wide) strips for binding.
- 14 (1½"-wide) strips. From strips, cut
  60 (1½" × 4½") D rectangles and 60
  (1½" × 3½") C rectangles.

Block Assembly

1. Join 1 B square, 1 matching E rect-
   angle, 1 matching F rectangle, 1 black
   print C rectangle, and 1 black print
   D rectangle as shown in *Block Unit
   Diagrams*. Make 2 matching Block
   Units.

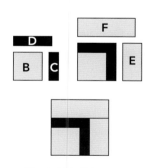

Block Unit Diagrams

2. Lay out Block Units, 2 matching A squares, 4 gray print F rectangles, and 1 black print G square as shown in *Block Assembly Diagram*. Join into rows; join rows to complete 1 block *(Block Diagram)*. Make 30 blocks.

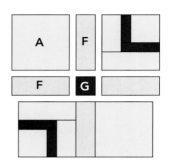

Block Assembly Diagram

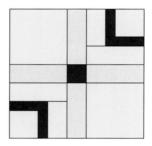

Block Diagram

Quilt Assembly

1. Lay out blocks as shown in *Quilt Top Assembly Diagram*.

2. Join blocks into rows; join rows to complete quilt top.

Finishing

1. Divide backing into 2 (2½-yard) lengths. Cut 1 piece in half lengthwise to make 2 narrow panels. Join 1 narrow panel to each side of wider panel; press seam allowances toward narrow panels.

2. Layer backing, batting, and quilt top; baste. Quilt as desired. Quilt shown was quilted with an allover design *(Quilting Diagram)*.

3. Join 2¼"-wide black print strips into 1 continuous piece for straight-grain French-fold binding. Add binding to quilt.

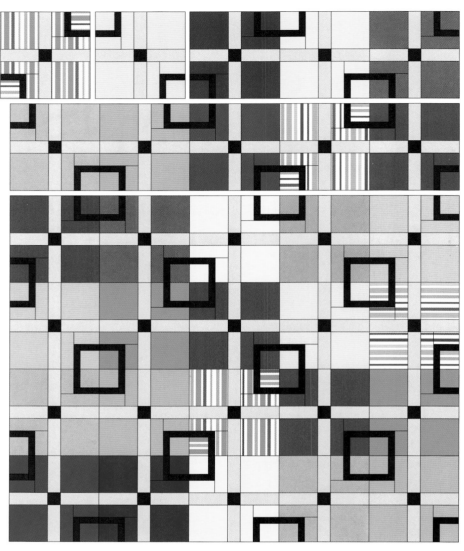

Quilt Top Assembly Diagram

Quilting Diagram

DESIGNER

Gudrun Erla was born and raised in Iceland. She has published several patterns and nine books, and is also a fabric designer. ✳

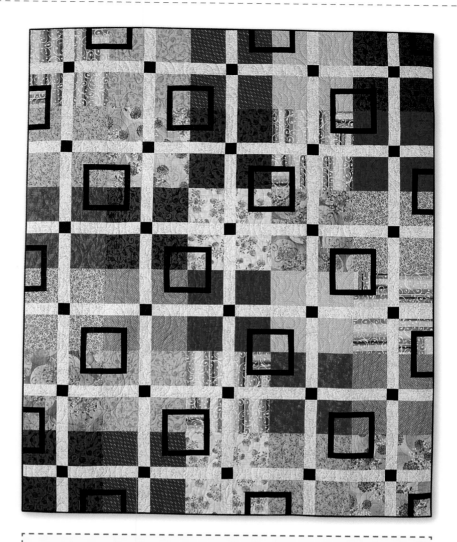

TRIED & TRUE

Our blocks are organic and earthy, yet modern and upscale, with a delicate dusting of gold metallic. The fabric collection is Earthtones by Norman Wyatt Jr./Art in Motion for P&B Textiles.

QUILT BY **Janine Burke.**
MACHINE QUILTED BY **Ann Davidson.**

Purple Haze

Bold blocks of color, each set in a contrasting frame, create a striking quilt that makes a powerful statement. A repetitive wave quilting pattern softens the strong graphic focus.

PROJECT RATING: EASY

Size: 85" × 80"

MATERIALS

½ yard **each** of 16 assorted solids in purple, gray, and teal

¾ yard purple solid for binding

7½ yards backing fabric

Full-size quilt batting

Cutting

Measurements include ¼" seam allowances.

From each ½ yard piece print, cut:

- 1 (8½"-wide) strip.
- 5 (1½"-wide) strips. Set aside 2 strips for strip sets. From remaining strips, cut 12 (1½" × 10½") A rectangles.

  NOTE: If fabric width has less than 42" of usable fabric, you will need to cut 6 (1½"-wide) strips.

From purple solid, cut:

- 9 (2¼"-wide) strips for binding.

Block Assembly

1. Join 1 (8½"-wide) strip and 2 (1½"-wide) strips as shown in *Strip Set Diagram*. Make 16 strip sets. From each strip set, cut:

- 1 (8½"-wide) #1 segment.
- 1 (7½"-wide) #2 segment.
- 1 (6½"-wide) #3 segment.
- 1 (5½"-wide) #4 segment.
- 1 (4½"-wide) #5 segment.
- 1 (3½"-wide) #6 segment.

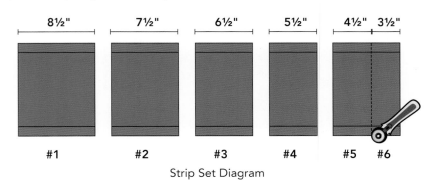

Strip Set Diagram

2. Add 2 matching A rectangles to 1 #1 segment as shown in *Block Assembly Diagram*. Make 16 blocks using #1 segments and matching A rectangles.

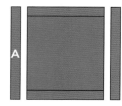

Block Assembly Diagram

3. In the same manner, make 16 blocks using #2 segments and matching A rectangles, 16 blocks using #3 segments and matching A rectangles, 16 blocks using #4 segments and matching A rectangles, 16 blocks using #5 segments and matching A rectangles, and 16 blocks using #6 segments and matching A rectangles (*Block Diagrams*).

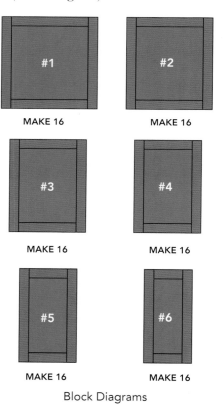

Block Diagrams

Quilt Assembly

1. Lay out blocks as shown in *Quilt Top Assembly Diagram*.
NOTE: The center row, which is the narrowest, only uses 8 of the 16 blocks of its size.

2. Join blocks into vertical rows; join rows to complete quilt top.

Finishing

1. Divide backing into 3 (2½-yard) lengths. Cut 1 piece in half lengthwise to make 2 narrow panels. Join 1 narrow panel to wider panels. Remaining panel is extra and can be used to make a hanging sleeve.

2. Layer backing, batting, and quilt top; baste. Quilt as desired. Quilt shown was quilted with an allover design (*Quilting Diagram*).

3. Join 2¼"-wide purple strips into 1 continuous piece for straight-grain French-fold binding. Add binding to quilt.

Quilting Diagram

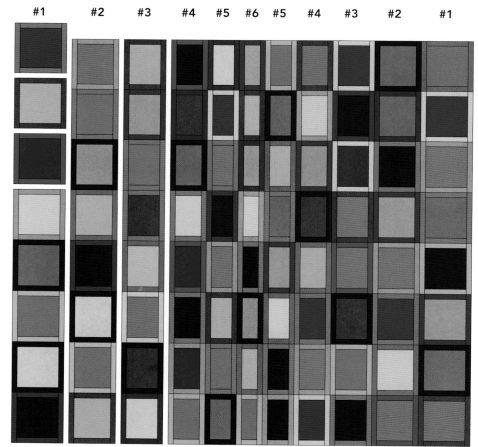

Quilt Top Assembly Diagram

DESIGNER

Janine Burke has been around needlework of some form for as long as she can remember. Inspired by her love of fabric and the graphics of everyday life, she designs from her home in the southwest suburbs of Chicago.

QUILT DESIGNED BY **Calli Taylor**.
MADE BY **Calli Taylor and Leslie Ison.** MACHINE QUILTED BY **Karen Morgan**.

Squares and Stripes

This quilt is easy to make and high in style. Choose your favorite bright color and combine it with black and white for an ultra modern look!

PROJECT RATING: EASY

Size: 65" × 81"

MATERIALS

2⅜ yards green print for stripes and binding
2¼ yards white solid for squares
2¼ yards black dot for squares
5 yards backing fabric
Twin-size quilt batting

Cutting

Measurements include ¼" seam allowances.

From green print, cut:

- 4 (5½"-wide) **lengthwise** strips. From strips, cut 4 (5½" × 81½") strips.
- 4 (2¼"-wide) **lengthwise** strips for binding.

From white solid, cut:

- 21 (3½"-wide) strips for strip sets.

From black dot, cut:

- 21 (3½"-wide) strips for strip sets.

Strip Set Row Assembly

1. Join 2 black dot strips and 1 white strip as shown in *Strip Set #1 Diagram*. Make 7 Strip Set #1. From strip sets, cut 68 (3½"-wide) #1 segments.

3½"

Strip Set #1 Diagram

2. In the same manner, join 2 white strips and 1 black dot strip as shown in *Strip Set #2 Diagram*. Make 7 Strip Set #2. From strip set, cut 67 (3½"-wide) #2 segments.

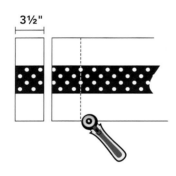

3½"

Strip Set #2 Diagram

3. Join 14 #1 segments and 13 #2 segments as shown in *Quilt Top Assembly Diagram* on page 30 to make 1 Row A. Make 3 Row A.

4. In the same manner, make 2 Row B using 14 #2 segments and 13 #1 segments in each.

Quilt Assembly

1. Lay out rows and green print strips as shown in *Quilt Top Assembly Diagram*.

2. Join rows and strips to complete quilt top.

Row A   **Row B**

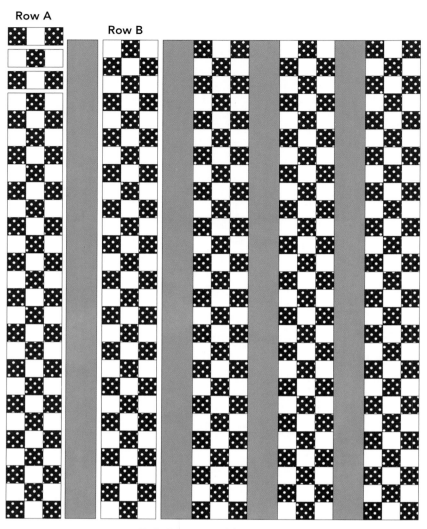

Quilt Top Assembly Diagram

Finishing

1. Divide backing into 2 (2½-yard) lengths. Cut 1 piece in half lengthwise to make 2 narrow panels. Join 1 narrow panel to each side of wider panel; press seam allowances toward narrow panels.

2. Layer backing, batting, and quilt top; baste. Quilt as desired. Quilt shown was quilted with an allover swirl design *(Quilting Diagram)*.

3. Join 2¼"-wide green print strips into 1 continuous piece for straight-grain French-fold binding. Add binding to quilt.

Quilting Diagram

DESIGNER

Calli Taylor's popular blog called Make it Do, shares quilting, sewing, cooking, and cleaning projects and tips. She writes about being resourceful and finding happiness in simple, everyday activities. ✳

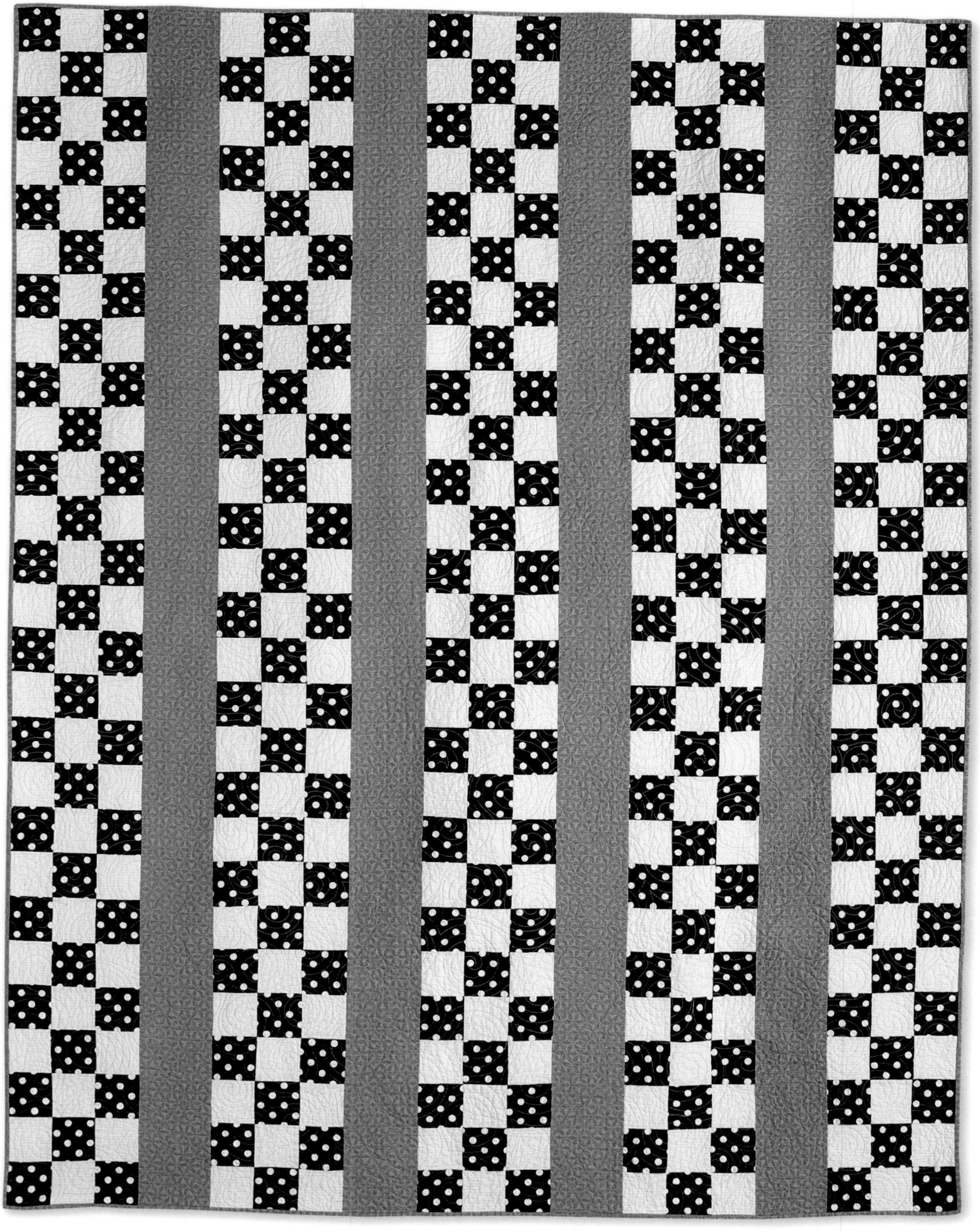

Urban Spaces

A collection of fabrics in neutral colors and stylized prints inspired Jean's quilt.
Easy to piece, you can finish it quickly with a simple geometric quilting design.

PROJECT RATING: EASY
Size: 63" × 84"
Blocks: 12 (21") blocks

MATERIALS

⅜ yard **each** of 12 assorted prints in
   black, cream, taupe, and gray
1⅜ yards cream print
1⅜ yards dark gray print
⅝ yard cream stripe for binding
5¼ yards backing fabric
Twin-size quilt batting

Cutting

Measurements include ¼" seam
allowances.

From each ⅜ yard piece, cut:

• 1 (6½"-wide) strip. From strip,
cut 1 (6½") B square, 2 (3½")
A squares, and 1 (2" × 15½")
D rectangle.

• 1 (5"-wide) strip. From strip,
cut 1 (5" × 15½") E rectangle
and 2 (5" × 9½") C rectangles.

From cream print, cut:

• 12 (3½"-wide) strips. From strips, cut
12 (3½" × 21½") G rectangles and 12
(3½" × 15½") F rectangles.

From dark gray print, cut:

• 12 (3½"-wide) strips. From strips, cut
12 (3½" × 21½") G rectangles and 12
(3½" × 15½") F rectangles.

From cream stripe, cut:

• 8 (2¼"-wide) strips for binding.

Block Assembly

1. Join 2 A squares, 1 B square, and 1
matching set of 2 C rectangles, 1 D
rectangle, and 1 E rectangle as shown
in *Block Center Diagrams*. Make 12
Block Centers.

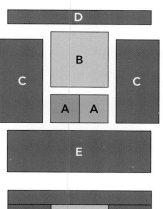

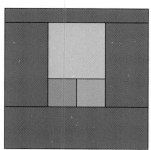

Block Center Diagrams

2. Add 2 cream print F rectangles and 2 cream print G rectangles to 1 Block Center as shown in *Block Assembly Diagram* to complete 1 cream block *(Block Diagrams)*. Make 6 cream blocks.

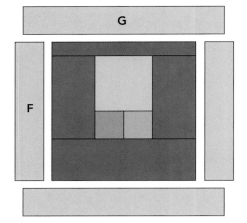

Block Assembly Diagram

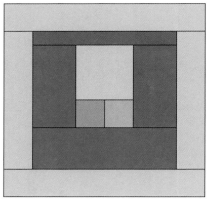

MAKE 6

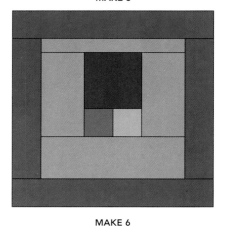

MAKE 6

Block Diagrams

3. In the same manner, make 6 gray blocks using 1 Block Center, 2 dark gray print F rectangles, and 2 dark gray print G rectangles in each.

Quilt Assembly

1. Lay out blocks as shown in *Quilt Top Assembly Diagram*.

2. Join blocks into rows; join rows to complete quilt top.

Finishing

1. Divide backing into 2 (2⅝-yard) lengths. Cut 1 piece in half lengthwise to make 2 narrow panels. Join 1 narrow panel to each side of wider panel; press seam allowances toward narrow panels.

1. Layer backing, batting, and quilt top; baste. Quilt as desired. Quilt shown was quilted with straight lines *(Quilting Diagram)*.

Quilt Top Assembly Diagram

2. Join 2¼"-wide white stripe strips into 1 continuous piece for straight-grain French-fold binding. Add binding to quilt.

Quilting Diagram

DESIGNER

Jean Nolte is the Editor of all Fons & Porter magazines and Editorial Director of "Love of Quilting" on public television. Quilting for nearly thirty years, she is always excited to try a new technique. Her fabric stash contains more yardage than she can possibly use in a lifetime, but she is having lots of fun trying. When not quilting, Jean loves to travel, knit, or spend time with her family.

Empire World

Make this Trip Around the World quilt in no time.
Big, easy-to-handle squares allow quick progress.

PROJECT RATING: EASY

Size: 96½" × 96½"

MATERIALS

1¾ yards dark red print
½ yard medium red print
½ yard red marbled print
⅜ yard dark gold print
¾ yard medium gold print
1¼ yards gold marbled print
¾ yard dark purple print
½ yard medium purple print
¾ yard purple marbled print
⅜ yard black-and-red print
⅜ yard black-and-gold print
¾ yard cream print
1 fat quarter★ gray print
2½ yards black solid
9 yards backing fabric
King-size quilt batting
★fat quarter = 18" × 20"

Cutting

Measurements include ¼" seam allowances. Border strips are exact length needed. You may want to cut them longer to allow for piecing variations.

From dark red print, cut:

- 11 (5"-wide) strips. From strips, cut 85 (5") squares.

From medium red print, cut:

- 3 (5"-wide) strips. From strips, cut 24 (5") squares.

From red marbled print, cut:

- 3 (5"-wide) strips. From strips, cut 20 (5") squares.

From dark gold print, cut:

- 2 (5"-wide) strips. From strips, cut 12 (5") squares.

From medium gold print, cut:

- 4 (5"-wide) strips. From strips, cut 32 (5") squares.

From gold marbled print, cut:

- 8 (5"-wide) strips. From strips, cut 60 (5") squares.

From dark purple print, cut:

- 4 (5"-wide) strips. From strips, cut 28 (5") squares.

From medium purple print, cut:

- 3 (5"-wide) strips. From strips, cut 24 (5") squares.

From purple marbled print, cut:

- 4 (5"-wide) strips. From strips, cut 28 (5") squares.

From black-and-red print, cut:

- 2 (5"-wide) strips. From strips, cut 16 (5") squares.

From black-and-gold print, cut:

- 2 (5"-wide) strips. From strips, cut 12 (5") squares.

From cream print, cut:

- 4 (5"-wide) strips. From strips, cut 32 (5") squares.

From gray print fat quarter, cut:

- 3 (5"-wide) strips. From strips, cut 8 (5") squares.

From black solid, cut:

- 8 (5"-wide) strips. From strips, cut 60 (5") squares.

- 11 (2¼"-wide) strips for binding.

- 10 (1½"-wide) strips. Piece strips to make 2 (1½" × 97") top and bottom borders and 2 (1½" × 95") side borders.

Quilt Assembly

1. Lay out squares as shown in *Quilt Top Assembly Diagram*.

2. Join into rows; join rows to complete quilt center.

3. Add black solid side borders to quilt center. Add top and bottom borders to quilt.

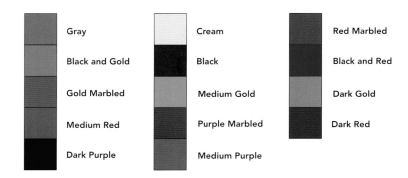

Quilt Top Assembly Diagram

Finishing

1. Divide backing into 3 (3-yard) lengths. Join panels lengthwise.

2. Layer backing, batting, and quilt top; baste. Quilt as desired. Quilt shown was quilted with an allover leaf design *(Quilting Diagram)*.

3. Join 2¼"-wide black solid strips into 1 continuous piece for straight-grain French-fold binding. Add binding to quilt.

Quilting Diagram

DESIGNER

Sisters Joanie Holton and Melanie Greseth grew up in the small Minnesota town of Brandon. For the past thirteen years, they have been designing and sewing samples to highlight the newest fabric lines for a variety of textile companies throughout the United States. Their business, Tailormade by Design, has provided them the opportunity to do what they love and work with fabulous people every day.

Gatsby

Soft aqua and chocolate hues in designs reminiscent of vintage wallpaper inspired editor Jean Nolte to create this quick and easy queen-size quilt.

PROJECT RATING: EASY

Size: 92" × 100"

Blocks: 42 (12") blocks

MATERIALS

4½ yards brown print #1 for blocks

3 yards brown print #2 for blocks, outer border, and binding

1⅜ yard green print for blocks and inner border

½ yard each of 4 assorted brown and aqua prints for blocks

8¼ yards backing fabric

King-size quilt batting

Cutting

Measurements include ¼" seam allowances. Border strips are exact length needed. You may want to make them longer to allow for piecing variations.

From brown print #1, cut:

• 12 (12½"-wide) strips. From strips, cut 42 (12½" × 8½") A rectangles and 7 (12½" × 4½") C rectangles.

From brown print #2, cut:

• 10 (6½"-wide) strips. Piece strips to make 2 (6½" × 92½") top and bottom outer borders and 2 (6½" × 88½") side outer borders.

• 3 (4½"-wide) strips. From strips, cut 21 (4½") B squares.

• 10 (2¼"-wide) strips for binding.

From green print, cut:

• 3 (4½"-wide) strips. From strips, cut 21 (4½") B squares.

• 9 (2½"-wide) strips. Piece strips to make 2 (2½" × 84½") side inner borders and 2 (2½" × 80½") top and bottom inner borders.

From each assorted print, cut:

• 3 (4½"-wide) strips. From strips, cut 21 (4½") B squares.

Block Assembly

1. Lay out 3 assorted B squares and 1 brown print #1 A rectangle as shown in *Block Assembly Diagram*.

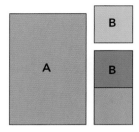

Block Assembly Diagram

2. Join pieces to make 1 block *(Block Diagram)*. Make 42 blocks.

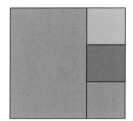

Block Diagram

Quilt Assembly

1. Lay out blocks and C rectangles as shown in *Quilt Top Assembly Diagram*. Join into rows; join rows to complete quilt center.
2. Add green print side inner borders to quilt center. Add top and bottom inner borders to quilt.
3. Repeat for brown print #2 outer borders.

Finishing

1. Divide backing into 3 (2¾-yard) lengths. Join panels lengthwise. Seams will run horizontally.
2. Layer backing, batting, and quilt top; baste. Quilt as desired. Quilt shown was quilted with parallel lines in the A rectangles and circles in the B squares and outer border *(Quilting Diagram)*.

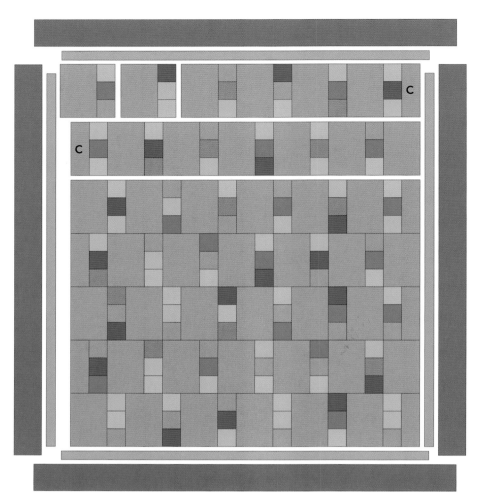

Quilt Top Assembly Diagram

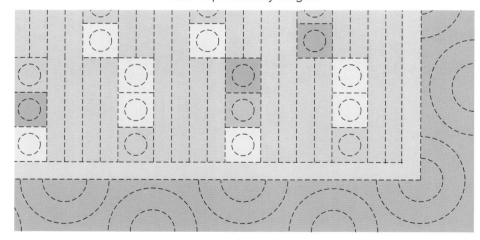

Quilting Diagram

3. Join 2¼"-wide brown print #2 strips into 1 continuous piece for straight-grain French-fold binding. Add binding to quilt.

French Farmhouse

Gail Kessler designed this quilt using subtle values of cream and taupe in an Irish Chain variation. Strip-piecing makes the block-making process quick and fun!

PROJECT RATING: EASY

Size: 97" × 97"

Blocks: 81 (10") blocks

MATERIALS

1 yard light cream print for blocks

1⅜ yards medium cream print for blocks

2⅜ yards cream stripe for blocks

1 yard light taupe print for blocks

3½ yards medium taupe print for blocks and border

1 yard dark taupe print for blocks

1 yard medium taupe check for blocks

2 yards dark taupe check for blocks and binding

9 yards backing fabric

King-size quilt batting

Cutting

Measurements include ¼" seam allowances. Border strips are exact length needed. You may want to make them longer to allow for piecing variations.

From light cream print, cut:

• 12 (2½"-wide) strips for strip sets.

From medium cream print, cut:

• 7 (6½"-wide) strips for strip sets.

From cream stripe, cut:

• 14 (2½"-wide) strips for strip sets.

From remaining cream stripe, cut:

• 5 (6½"-wide) **lengthwise** strips for strip sets.

From light taupe print, cut:

• 12 (2½"-wide) strips for strip sets.

From medium taupe print, cut:

• 11 (4"-wide) strips. Piece strips to make 2 (4" × 97½") top and bottom borders and 2 (4" × 90½") side borders.

• 24 (2½"-wide) strips for strip sets.

From dark taupe print, cut:

• 12 (2½"-wide) strips for strip sets.

From medium taupe check, cut:

• 10 (2½"-wide) strips for strip sets.

From dark taupe check, cut:

• 15 (2½"-wide) strips for strip sets.

• 11 (2¼"-wide) strips for binding.

Block Assembly

1. Join 2 dark taupe check strips, 2 medium taupe print strips, and 1 light cream print strip as shown in *Strip Set #1 Diagram*. Make 6 strip set #1. From strip sets, cut 82 (2½"-wide) #1 segments.

Sew **Smart**™

When joining strips for strip sets, alternate sewing direction from strip to strip. This keeps strip sets straight. —Marianne

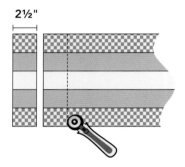

Strip Set #1 Diagram

2. Join 2 medium taupe print strips, 2 dark taupe print strips, and 1 light taupe print strip as shown in *Strip Set #2 Diagram*. Make 6 Strip Set #2. From strip sets, cut 82 (2½"-wide) #2 segments.

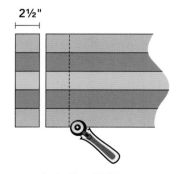

Strip Set #2 Diagram

3. Join 2 light cream print strips, 2 light taupe print strips, and 1 dark taupe check strip as shown in *Strip Set #3 Diagram*. Make 3 Strip Set #3. From strip sets, cut 41 (2½"-wide) #3 segments.

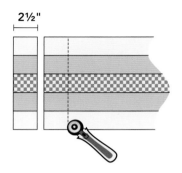

Strip Set #3 Diagram

4. Join 2 (2½"-wide) cream stripe strips and 1 medium cream print strip as shown in *Strip Set #4 Diagram*. Make 7 Strip Set #4. From strip sets, cut 40 (6½"-wide) #4 segments.

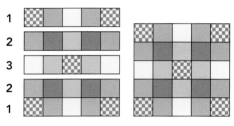

Strip Set #4 Diagram

5. Join 2 medium taupe check strips and 1 (6½"-wide) cream stripe strip as shown in *Strip Set #5 Diagram*. Make 5 Strip Set #5. From strip sets, cut 80 (2½"-wide) #5 segments.

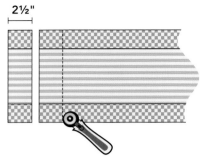

Strip Set #5 Diagram

6. Lay out 2 #1 segments, 2 #2 segments, and 1 #3 segment as shown in *Block A Diagrams*. Join segments to complete 1 Block A. Make 41 Block A.

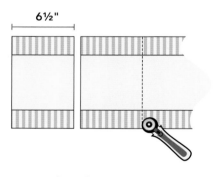

Block A Diagrams

7. Lay out 2 #5 segments and 1 #4 segment as shown in *Block B Diagrams*. Join segments to complete 1 Block B. Make 40 Block B.

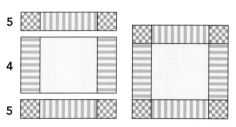

Block B Diagrams

Quilt Assembly

1. Lay out blocks as shown in *Quilt Top Assembly Diagram* on page 47.

2. Join into rows; join rows to complete quilt center.

3. Add medium taupe print side borders to quilt center. Add top and bottom borders to quilt.

Quilt Top Assembly Diagram

Finishing

1. Divide backing into 3 (3-yard) lengths. Join panels lengthwise.

2. Layer backing, batting, and quilt top; baste. Quilt as desired. Quilt shown was quilted with a diagonal grid through the blocks and a leaf design in the border (*Quilting Diagram*).

3. Join 2¼"-wide dark taupe check strips into 1 continuous piece for straight-grain French-fold binding. Add binding to quilt.

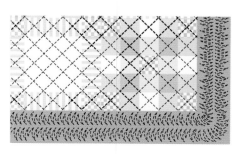

Quilting Diagram

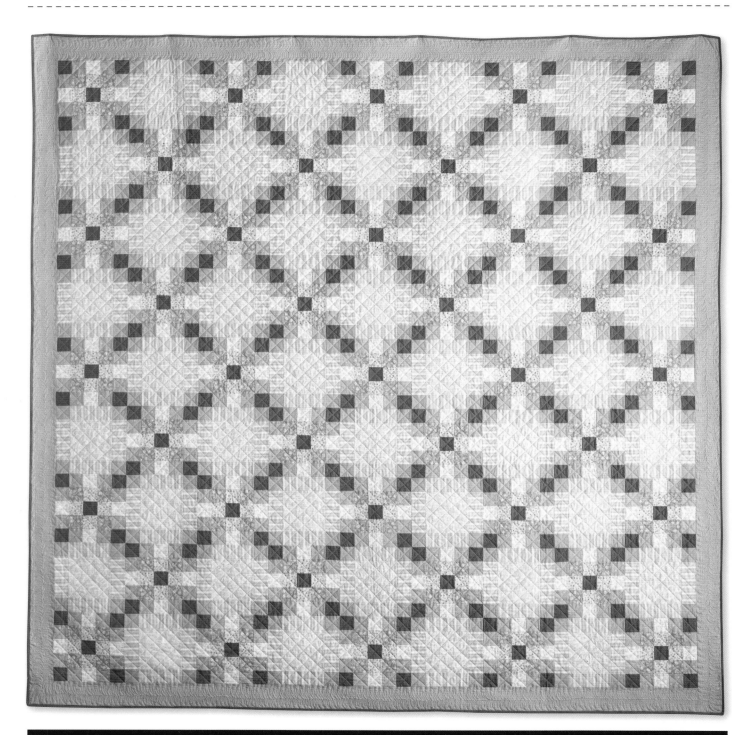

DESIGNER

Gail Kessler owns Ladyfingers Sewing Studio in Oley, Pennsylvania, and is also a fabric designer.

SIZE OPTIONS

	Crib (37" × 47")	Throw (47" × 67")	Twin (57" × 97")
Block 1	6	12	23
Block 2	6	12	22
Setting	3 × 4	4 × 6	5 × 9

MATERIALS

	Crib (37" × 47")	Throw (47" × 67")	Twin (57" × 97")
Light Cream Print	¼ yard	⅜ yard	1 yard
Medium Cream Print	¼ yard	½ yard	⅞ yard
Cream Stripe	1⅜ yards	1½ yards	1¾ yards
Light Taupe Print	¼ yard	⅜ yard	⅝ yard
Medium Taupe Print	1 yard	1½ yards	2 yards
Dark Taupe Print	¼ yard	⅜ yard	½ yard
Medium Taupe Check	¼ yard	⅜ yard	½ yard
Dark Taupe Check	⅝ yard	1 yard	1¼ yards
Backing Fabric	1½ yards	3 yards	6 yards
Batting	Crib-size	Twin-size	Queen-size

Web **Extra**

Go to FonsandPorter.com/farmhousesizes to download *Quilt Top Assembly Diagrams* for these size options.

TRIED & TRUE

Whimsical blooms and stripes in pink and chocolate enrich our colorful variation. Fabrics are from the California Calico collection by Timeless Treasures.

Star-Spangled Beauty

Patriotic stars and stripes are combined into a generously sized Quilt of Valor.

PROJECT RATING: EASY

Size: 72" × 86"

Blocks: 50 (6") Star blocks

MATERIALS

3⅛ yards white print for blocks

2¼ yards red print for sashing and border

1½ yards red stripe for sashing and binding

1 yard light blue print for blocks

1 yard dark blue print for blocks

6¾ yards backing fabric

Twin-size quilt batting

Cutting

Measurements include ¼" seam allowances. Border strips are exact length needed. You may want to cut them longer to allow for piecing variations.

From white print, cut:

• 3 (8½"-wide) strips. From strips, cut 45 (8½" × 2½") E rectangles.

• 4 (6½"-wide) strips. From strips, cut 50 (6½" × 2½") D rectangles.

• 10 (3½"-wide) strips. From strips, cut 200 (3½" × 2") C rectangles.

• 10 (2"-wide) strips. From strips, cut 200 (2") A squares.

From red print, cut:

• 4 (4½"-wide) **lengthwise** strips. From strips, cut 2 (4½" × 78½") side borders and 2 (4½" × 72½") top and bottom borders.

• 8 (2½"-wide) **lengthwise** strips. From strips, cut 8 (2½" × 78½") sashing strips.

From red stripe, cut:

• 9 (2½"-wide) strips. Piece strips to make 4 (2½" × 78½") sashing strips.

• 9 (2¼"-wide) strips for binding.

From light blue print, cut:

• 3 (3½"-wide) strips. From strips, cut 25 (3½") B squares.

• 10 (2"-wide) strips. From strips, cut 200 (2") A squares.

From dark blue print, cut:

• 3 (3½"-wide) strips. From strips, cut 25 (3½") B squares.

• 10 (2"-wide) strips. From strips, cut 200 (2") A squares.

Star Block Assembly

1. Referring to *Star Point Unit Diagrams*, place 1 light blue print A square atop 1 white print C rectangle, right sides facing. Stitch diagonally from corner to corner as shown. Trim ¼" beyond stitching. Press open to reveal triangle. Repeat for opposite end of rectangle to complete 1 Star Point Unit. Make 100 light blue Star Point Units.

Star Point Unit Diagrams

2. In the same manner, make 100 dark blue Star Point Units using dark blue print A squares and white print C rectangles.

3. Lay out 4 light blue Star Point Units, 4 white print A squares, and 1 light blue print B square as shown in *Block Assembly Diagram*. Join into rows; join rows to complete 1 light blue block *(Block Diagrams)*. Make 25 light blue blocks. In the same manner, make 25 dark blue blocks.

Block Assembly Diagram

MAKE 25   **MAKE 25**

Block Diagrams

4. Add 1 white print D rectangle to each block as shown in *Block Unit Diagram*. Make 50 Block Units.

Block Unit Diagram

Quilt Assembly

1. Referring to *Quilt Top Assembly Diagram*, join 10 Block Units and 9 white print E rectangles to make 1 Block row. Make 5 Block rows.

2. Join 2 red print sashing strips and 1 stripe sashing strip to make 1 Sashing row. Make 4 Sashing rows.

3. Join rows as shown to complete quilt center.

4. Add side borders to quilt center. Add top and bottom borders to quilt.

Quilt Top Assembly Diagram

Finishing

1. Divide backing into 3 (2¼-yard) lengths. Cut 1 piece in half lengthwise to make 2 narrow panels. Join 1 narrow panel to wider panels. Remaining panel is extra.

2. Layer backing, batting, and quilt top; baste. Quilt as desired. Quilt shown was quilted with meandering loops in block row background, wavy lines in sashing rows, and stars in border *(Quilting Diagram)*.

3. Join 2¼"-wide red stripe strips into 1 continuous piece for straight-grain French-fold binding. Add binding to quilt.

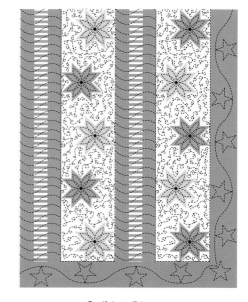

Quilting Diagram

DESIGNER

Debra Finan sews and knits with equal enthusiasm, and always has several projects in the works.

QUILT BY **Janet Houts**.
MACHINE QUILTED BY **Margie Kraft**.

Venetian Dream

Window and floor designs in Venice were designer Janet Houts' inspiration for this dramatic quilt.

PROJECT RATING: EASY

Size: 57" × 73"

Blocks: 12 (15") blocks

MATERIALS

1 yard large-scale red print for blocks

½ yard medium-scale red print for blocks

¾ yard dark red print for blocks and binding

1 fat quarter★ light green print for blocks

¾ yard dark green print for blocks

1½ yards cream print for blocks and sashing

1 yard red stripe for border

3½ yards backing fabric

Twin-size quilt batting

★fat quarter = 18" × 20"

Cutting

Measurements include ¼" seam allowances. Border strips are exact length needed. You may want to make them longer to allow for piecing variations.

From large-scale red print, cut:

• 3 (9½"-wide) strips. From strips, cut 12 (9½") D squares.

From medium-scale red print, cut:

• 2 (6½"-wide) strips. From strips, cut 12 (6½") C squares.

From dark red print, cut:

• 2 (2½"-wide) strips. From strips, cut 24 (2½") A squares.

• 8 (2¼"-wide) strips for binding.

From light green print fat quarter, cut:

• 4 (2½"-wide) strips. From strips, cut 24 (2½") A squares.

From dark green print, cut:

• 4 (5½"-wide) strips. From strips, cut 24 (5½") B squares.

From cream print, cut:

• 30 (1½"-wide) strips. Piece 7 strips to make 5 (1½" × 49½") horizontal sashing strips. From remaining strips, cut 16 (1½" × 15½") vertical sashing strips, 24 (1½" × 9½") G rectangles, 48 (1½" × 5½") F rectangles, and 24 (1½" × 2½") E rectangles.

From red stripe, cut:

• 7 (4½"-wide) strips. Piece strips to make 2 (4½" × 65½") side borders and 2 (4½" × 57½") top and bottom borders.

Block Assembly

1. Lay out 1 light green print A square, 1 dark red print A square, 1 dark green print B square, 1 cream print E rectangle, 2 cream print F rectangles, and 1 cream print G rectangle as shown in *Unit 1 Diagrams.* Join to complete 1 Unit 1. Make 12 Unit 1.

Unit 1 Diagrams

2. Lay out 1 light green print A square, 1 dark red print A square, 1 dark green print B square, 1 cream print E rectangle, 2 cream print F rectangles, and 1 cream print G rectangle as shown in *Unit 2 Diagrams.* Join to complete 1 Unit 2. Make 12 Unit 2.

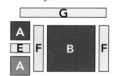 

Unit 2 Diagrams

3. Lay out 1 Unit 1, 1 Unit 2, 1 medium-scale red print C square, and 1 large-scale red print D square as shown in *Block Diagrams.* Join to complete 1 block. Make 12 blocks.

Quilt Assembly

1. Lay out blocks and cream print sashing strips as shown in *Quilt Top Assembly Diagram.* Join into rows; join rows to complete quilt center.

2. Add side borders to quilt center. Add top and bottom borders to quilt.

Finishing

1. Divide backing into 2 (1¾-yard) lengths. Join panels lengthwise. Seam will run horizontally.

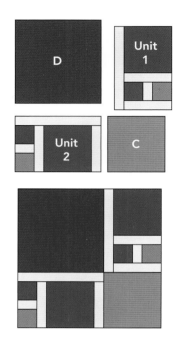

Block Diagrams

2. Layer backing, batting, and quilt top; baste. Quilt as desired. Quilt shown was quilted with an allover floral design *(Quilting Diagram).*

3. Join 2¼"-wide dark red print strips into 1 continuous piece for straight-grain French-fold binding. Add binding to quilt.

Quilting Diagram

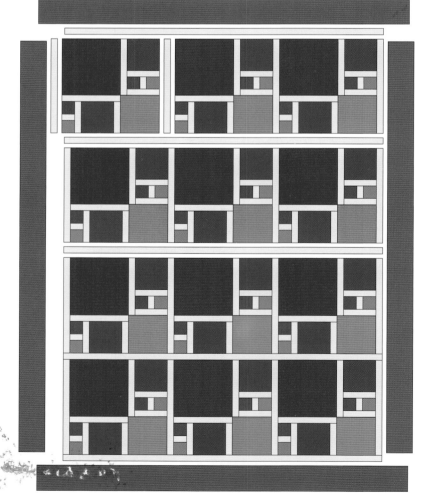

Quilt Top Assembly Diagram

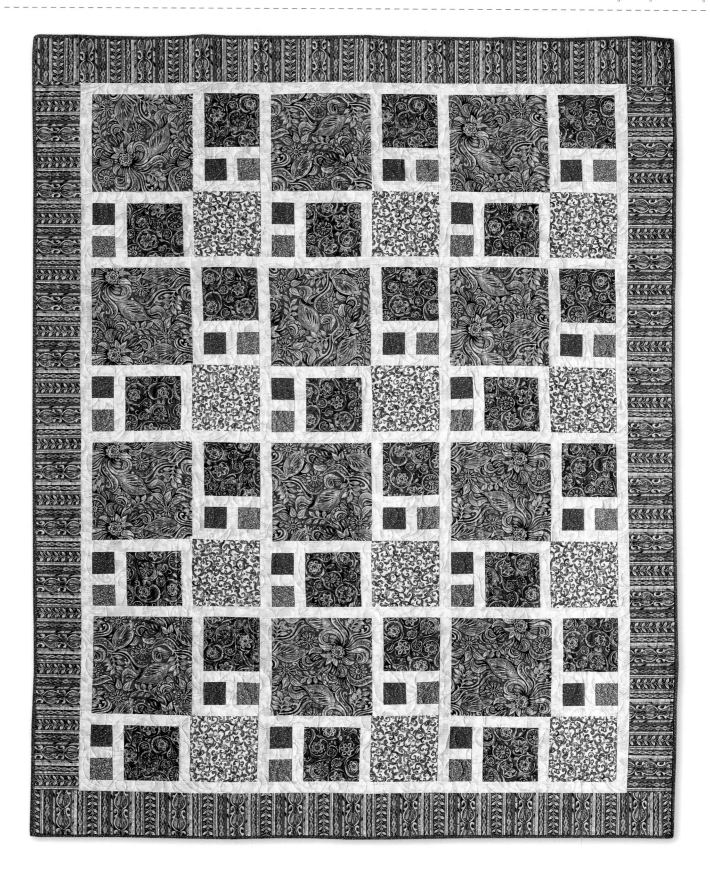

SIZE OPTIONS

	Crib (41" × 41")	Full (73" × 89")	Queen (89" × 105")
Blocks	4	20	30
Setting	2 × 2	4 × 5	5 × 6

MATERIALS

	Crib	Full	Queen
Large-scale Red Print	⅜ yard	1½ yards	2¼ yards
Medium-scale Red Print	¼ yard	⅞ yard	1 yard
Dark Red Print	½ yard	1 yard	1⅛ yards
Light Green Print	1 fat eighth★	⅜ yard	⅜ yard
Dark Green Print	⅜ yard	1 yard	1½ yards
Cream Print	⅝ yard	2¼ yards	3⅛ yards
Red Stripe	¾ yard	1⅛ yards	1⅜ yards
Backing Fabric	2½ yards	5¼ yards	7⅞ yards
Batting	Crib-size	Full-size	Queen-size

★fat eighth = 9" × 20"

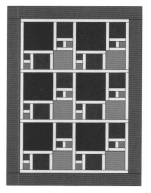

Crib Size

Full Size

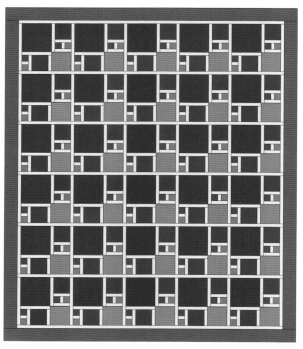

Queen Size

TRIED & TRUE

Babies and toddlers will love a quilt made with these bright prints from Michael Miller.

DESIGNER

Janet Houts began quilting nine years ago, and now designs quilts for Blank Quilting. Janet resides in Sun Valley, Idaho, where she draws inspiration from her beautiful surroundings.

Watermelon & Shoofly

With its country color scheme and fun Watermelon and Shoofly blocks, this quilt reminds us of a summer picnic.

PROJECT RATING: EASY
Size: 42" × 56"
Blocks: 11 (13" × 6") Watermelon blocks
13 (6") Shoofly blocks

MATERIALS

8 fat quarters★ assorted red prints and plaids for Watermelon blocks and outer border

4 fat eighths★★ assorted green prints for Watermelon blocks

8 fat eighths★★ assorted prints in gold, red, blue, and black for Shoofly blocks

¾ yard cream print for block backgrounds

⅞ yard black plaid for sashing and inner border

Fons & Porter Half & Quarter Ruler (optional)

8" square black wool or felt for watermelon seeds

5 yards ⅜"-wide cream rickrack

½ yard red print for binding

2¾ yards backing fabric

Crib-size quilt batting

★fat quarter = 18" × 20"

★★fat eighth = 9" × 20"

Cutting

Measurements include ¼" seam allowances. Border strips are exact length needed. You may want to make them longer to allow for piecing variations. Pattern for Seed is on page 63. Instructions are written for using the Fons & Porter Half & Quarter Ruler. For instructions on using this ruler, go to FonsandPorter.com/hqr. If not using this ruler, follow cutting Notes.

From each of three red fat quarters, cut:

• 2 (5½"-wide) strips. From strips, cut 2 (5½" × 11½") A rectangles.

From each of five red fat quarters, cut:

• 1 (5½"-wide) strip. From strip, cut 1 (5½" × 11½") A rectangle.

From remainders of red fat quarters, cut a total of:

• 14 (3½" × 8½") H rectangles.

• 12 (3½" × 6½") G rectangles.

From each green print fat eighth, cut:

• 5 (1½"-wide) strips. From strips, cut 3 (1½" × 13½") C rectangles, 6 (1½" × 5½") D rectangles, and 6 (1½") B squares.

From each assorted print fat eighth, cut:

• 2 (2½"-wide) strips. From strips, cut 2 (2½") E squares and 7 half-square F triangles. (You will have a few extra.)

NOTE: If not using the Fons & Porter Half & Quarter Ruler to cut the F triangles, cut 1 (2⅞"-wide) strip. From strip, cut 4 (2⅞") squares. Cut squares in half diagonally to make 8 half-square F triangles.

From cream print, cut:

• 7 (2½"-wide) strips. From strips, cut 52 (2½") E squares and 52 half-square F triangles.

NOTE: If not using the Fons & Porter Half & Quarter Ruler to cut the F triangles, cut 2 (2⅞"-wide) strips. From strips, cut 26 (2⅞") squares. Cut squares in half diagonally to make 52 half-square F triangles.

• 2 (1½"-wide) strips. From strips, cut 22 (1½") B squares.

From black plaid, cut:

• 18 (1½"-wide) strips. From 15 strips, cut 2 (1½" × 34½") top and bottom inner borders, 6 (1½" × 34½") horizontal sashing rectangles, and 17 (1½" × 6½") vertical sashing rectangles. Piece remaining strips to make 2 (1½" × 50½") side inner borders.

From red print, cut:

• 6 (2¼"-wide) strips for binding.

From black wool, cut:

• 55 Seeds.

Watermelon Block Assembly

1. Referring to *Diagonal Seams Diagrams*, place 1 green print B square atop 1 red print A rectangle, right sides facing. Stitch diagonally from corner to corner as shown. Trim ¼" beyond stitching. Press open to reveal triangle. Repeat for opposite end of rectangle to complete 1 Watermelon Unit.

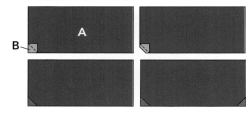

Diagonal Seams Diagrams

2. In the same manner, make 1 Rind Unit using cream print B squares and green print C rectangle *(Rind Unit Diagram)*.

Rind Unit Diagram

3. Lay out Watermelon Unit, Rind Unit, and 2 matching green print D rectangles as shown in *Watermelon Block Assembly Diagram*. Join to complete 1 Watermelon block *(Watermelon Block Diagram)*.

Watermelon Block Assembly Diagram

Watermelon Block Diagram

4. Position 5 seeds atop Watermelon block. Appliqué seeds in place.

5. Make 11 Watermelon blocks.

Shoofly Block Assembly

1. Join 1 cream print F triangle and 1 print F triangle as shown in *Triangle-Square Diagrams*. Make 13 sets of 4 matching triangle-squares.

Triangle-Square Diagrams

2. Lay out 1 set of triangle-squares, 1 matching print E square, and 4 cream print E squares as shown in *Shoofly Block Assembly Diagram*. Join into rows; join rows to complete 1 Shoofly block *(Shoofly Block Diagram)*. Make 13 Shoofly blocks.

Shoofly Block Assembly Diagram

Shoofly Block Diagram

Outer Border Assembly

1. Join 7 assorted red print H rectangles as shown in *Quilt Top Assembly Diagram* on page 63 to make 1 side outer border. Make 2 side outer borders.

2. In the same manner, make top and bottom outer borders, using 6 assorted red print G rectangles in each.

Quilt Assembly

1. Lay out blocks and sashing rectangles as shown in *Quilt Top Assembly Diagram*. Join into rows; join rows to complete quilt center.

2. Add top and bottom inner borders to quilt center. Add side inner borders to quilt.

Quilt Top Assembly Diagram

DESIGNER

Tammy Johnson is half of the design duo, Joined at the Hip. Tammy and Avis Shirer have been designing quilts since 1997. They have self-published hundreds of patterns and thirteen books, and have also done work for That Patchwork Place and Kansas City Star. They love to combine piecing and appliqué in their whimsical designs. The duo has also designed several lines of fabric for Clothworks Textiles. Their love of nature and the changing seasons in Iowa are reflected in their patterns and fabric designs.

Seed

3. Repeat for pieced outer borders.

4. Stitch rickrack to quilt top, covering seam between inner and outer borders.

Finishing

1. Divide backing into 2 (1⅜-yard) lengths. Join panels lengthwise. Seam will run horizontally.

2. Layer backing, batting, and quilt top; baste. Quilt as desired. Quilt shown was quilted in the ditch, with wavy lines in sashing, and with Xs in outer border *(Quilting Diagram)*.

3. Join 2¼"-wide red print strips into 1 continuous piece for straight-grain French-fold binding. Add binding to quilt.

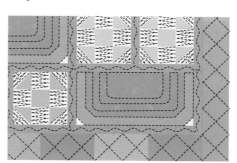

Quilting Diagram

Patriotic Patchwork

Debra designed this quilt by accident! She started out with an idea for a Jacob's ladder quilt, changed her mind, started another design, changed her mind again, and ended up with this design. It's now one of her favorite scrap quilts.

PROJECT RATING: EASY

Size: 72" × 72"

Blocks: 81 (8") Double
Four Patch blocks

MATERIALS

8 fat quarters★ assorted dark prints
   in blue and black
8 fat quarters★ assorted red prints
14 fat quarters★ assorted light prints
   in cream, beige, and tan
⅝ yard black print for binding
4½ yards backing fabric
Full-size quilt batting
★fat quarter = 18" × 20"

Cutting

Measurements include ¼" seam allowances.

From assorted dark print fat quarters, cut a total of:

• 10 (4½"-wide) strips. From strips, cut 40 (4½") squares.
• 24 (2½"-wide) strips for strip sets.

From assorted red print fat quarters, cut a total of:

• 11 (4½"-wide) strips. From strips, cut 41 (4½") squares.
• 23 (2½"-wide) strips for strip sets.

From assorted light print fat quarters, cut a total of:

• 21 (4½"-wide) strips. From strips, cut 81 (4½") squares.
• 47 (2½"-wide) strips for strip sets.

From black print, cut:

• 8 (2¼"-wide) strips for binding.

Block Assembly

1. Join 1 light print strip and 1 dark or red print strip as shown in *Strip Set Diagram*. Make 47 strip sets. From strip sets, cut 324 (2½"-wide) segments.

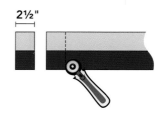

Strip Set Diagram

2. Join 2 segments as shown in *Four Patch Unit Diagrams*. Make 162 Four Patch Units.

Four Patch Unit Diagrams

3. Lay out 1 red print square, 1 light print square, and 2 Four Patch Units. Join into rows; join rows to complete 1 red block *(Block Diagrams)*. Make 41 red blocks.

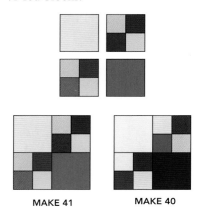

MAKE 41   MAKE 40

Block Diagrams

4. In the same manner, make 40 dark blocks using 1 dark print square, 1 light print square, and 2 Four Patch Units in each.

Quilt Assembly

1. Lay out blocks as shown in *Quilt Top Assembly Diagram.*

2. Join into rows; join rows to complete quilt top.

Finishing

1. Divide backing into 2 (2¼-yard) lengths. Cut 1 piece in half lengthwise to make 2 narrow panels. Join 1 narrow panel to each side of wider panel; press seam allowances toward narrow panels.

2. Layer backing, batting, and quilt top; baste. Quilt as desired. Quilt shown was quilted with allover meandering *(Quilting Diagram).*

3. Join 2¼"-wide black print strips into 1 continuous piece for straight-grain French-fold binding. Add binding to quilt.

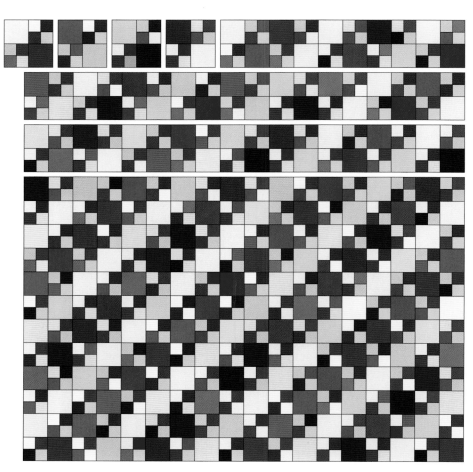

Quilt Top Assembly Diagram

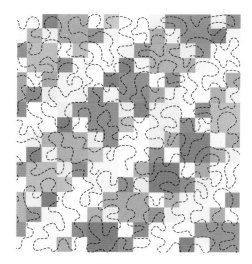

Quilting Diagram

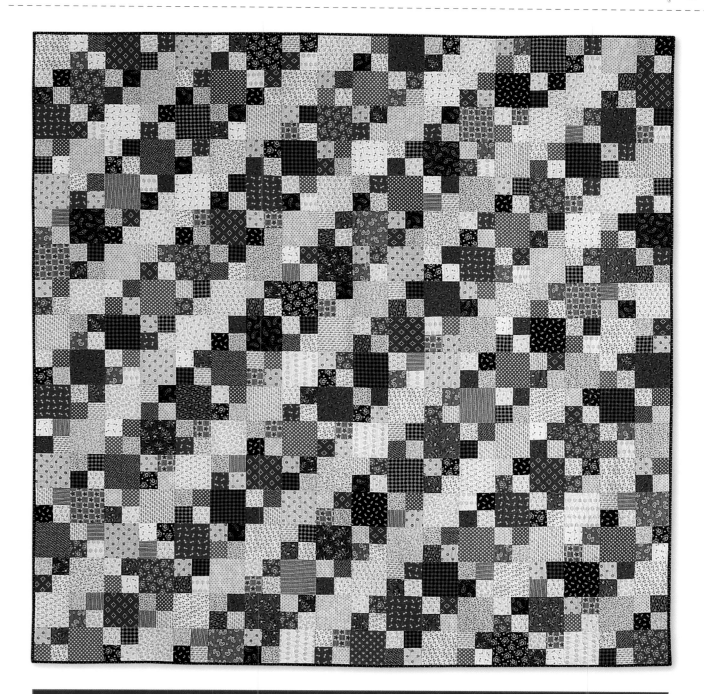

DESIGNER

Debra Finan is the Managing Editor for all Fons & Porter titles. She sews and knits with equal enthusiasm, and always has several projects in the works.

Jazzy Cats

The cool cats on this fun quilt are sure to make any music lover smile.
It's easy to piece using our quick diagonal seams method.

PROJECT RATING: EASY

Size: 74" × 98"

Blocks: 18 (12") Music Note blocks
17 (12") Puss in the Corner blocks

MATERIALS

2¼ yards white print
2 yards black print
¾ yard yellow print
2¾ yards blue print
1½ yards stripe
6 yards backing fabric
Queen-size quilt batting

Cutting

Measurements include ¼" seam allowances. Border strips are exact length needed. You may want to make them longer to allow for piecing variations.

From white print, cut:

- 6 (3½"-wide) strips. From strips, cut 18 (3½" × 6½") I rectangles and 18 (3½" × 5½") G rectangles.
- 3 (2½"-wide) strips. From strips, cut 18 (2½" × 4½") J rectangles.
- 30 (1½"-wide) strips. From strips, cut 36 (1½" × 12½") L rectangles, 36 (1½" × 10½") K rectangles, and 144 (1½") D squares.

From black print, cut:

- 5 (4½"-wide) strips. From strips, cut 36 (4½") E squares.
- 4 (3½"-wide) strips. From strips, cut 18 (3½" × 7½") F rectangles.
- 10 (2¼"-wide) strips for binding.
- 4 (1½"-wide) strips. From strips, cut 36 (1½" × 3½") H rectangles.

From yellow print, cut:

- 8 (2½"-wide) strips. Piece strips to make 2 (2½" × 84½") side inner borders and 2 (2½" × 64½") top and bottom inner borders.

From blue print, cut:

- 3 (6½"-wide) strips. From strips, cut 17 (6½") A squares.
- 9 (5½"-wide) strips. Piece strips to make 2 (5½" × 88½") side inner borders and 2 (5½" × 74½") top and bottom inner borders.
- 7 (3½"-wide) strips. From strips, cut 68 (3½") B squares.

From stripe, cut:

- 12 (3½"-wide) strips, centering design in each. From strips, cut 68 (3½" × 6½") C rectangles.

Block Assembly

1. Lay out 1 blue print A square, 4 blue print B squares, and 4 stripe C rectangles as shown in *Puss in the Corner Block Diagrams*. Join into rows; join rows to complete 1 Puss in the Corner block. Make 17 Puss in the Corner blocks.

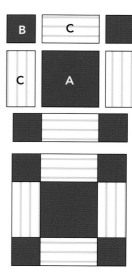

Puss in the Corner Block Diagrams

2. Referring to *Diagonal Seams Diagrams*, place 1 white print D square atop 1 black print E square, right sides facing. Stitch diagonally from corner to corner as shown. Trim ¼" beyond stitching. Press open to reveal triangle. Repeat on 2 more corners to complete 1 Unit 1 *(Unit 1 Diagram)*. Make 36 Unit 1.

Diagonal Seams Diagrams

Unit 1 Diagram

3. Using diagonal seams method, stitch 2 white print D squares to 1 black print F rectangle as shown in *Unit 2 Diagrams*. Make 18 Unit 2.

Unit 2 Diagrams

4. Lay out 1 white print G rectangle and 2 black print H rectangles as shown in *Unit 3 Diagrams*. Join to complete 1 Unit 3. Make 18 Unit 3.

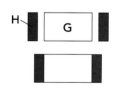

Unit 3 Diagrams

5. Lay out 2 Unit 1, 1 Unit 2, 1 Unit 3, 1 white print I rectangle, 1 white print J rectangle, 2 white print K rectangles, and 2 white print L rectangles as shown in *Note Block Assembly Diagrams*. Join to complete 1 Note block *(Note Block Diagram)*. Make 18 Note blocks.

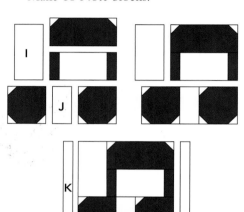

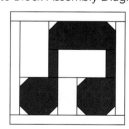

Note Block Assembly Diagrams

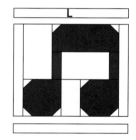

Note Block Diagram

Quilt Assembly

1. Lay out blocks as shown in *Quilt Top Assembly Diagram* on page 71. Join into rows; join rows to complete quilt center.

2. Add yellow print side inner borders to quilt center. Add yellow print top and bottom inner borders to quilt.

3. Repeat for blue print outer borders.

Finishing

1. Divide backing into 2 (3-yard) lengths. Cut 1 piece in half lengthwise to make 2 narrow panels. Join 1 narrow panel to each side of wider panel; press seam allowances toward narrow panels.

2. Layer backing, batting, and quilt top; baste. Quilt as desired. Quilt shown was quilted with allover meandering *(Quilting Diagram)*.

3. Join 2¼"-wide black print strips into 1 continuous piece for straight-grain French-fold binding. Add binding to quilt

Quilting Diagram

Quilt Top Assembly Diagram

TRIED & TRUE

Cowboys and cowgirls love music too!
We used bright prints from the Horsing Around collection
by Desiree's Designs for Red Rooster Fabrics.

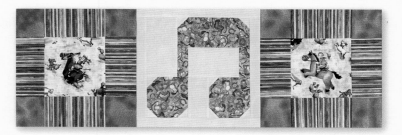

Happy Howling

It's fun to use a collection of holiday-themed prints in your quilt. Designer Florence Moy made this quilt using Halloween prints, but her pattern would also work well for Christmas, Valentine's Day, or even a birthday celebration quilt.

PROJECT RATING: EASY

Size: 51" × 61"

Blocks: 80 (4") blocks

MATERIALS

80 (4½") (A) squares in assorted theme prints

2¼ yards white print for sashing and outer border

½ yard black solid for inner border

⅜ yard orange solid for middle border

½ yard black print for binding

Assorted scraps for appliqué (optional)

Paper-backed fusible web (optional)

3¼ yards backing fabric

Twin-size quilt batting

Cutting

Measurements include ¼" seam allowances. Border strips are exact length needed. You may want to make them longer to allow for piecing variations. Patterns for optional appliqué shapes are on page 74. Follow manufacturer's instructions if using fusible web.

From white print, cut:
- 6 (5"-wide) strips. Piece strips to make 2 (5" × 52½") side outer borders and 2 (5" × 51½") top and bottom outer borders.
- 6 (4½"-wide) strips. From strips, cut 142 (4½" × 1½") sashing rectangles.
- 13 (1½"-wide) strips. From strips, cut 320 (1½") B squares.

From black solid, cut:
- 7 (1½"-wide) strips. From 2 strips, cut 31 (1½") B squares. Piece remaining strips to make 2 (1½" × 49½") side inner borders and 2 (1½" × 41½") top and bottom inner borders.

From orange solid, cut:
- 2 (1½"-wide) strips. From strips, cut 32 (1½") B squares.
- 5 (1"-wide) strips. Piece strips to make 2 (1" × 51½") side middle borders and 2 (1" × 42½") top and bottom middle borders.

From black print, cut:
- 6 (2¼"-wide) strips for binding.

Optional Border Appliqué

From assorted scraps, cut:

• Appliqué pieces.

From orange solid, cut:

• 8 C squares.

From black solid, cut:

• 8 C squares.

Block Assembly

1. Referring to *Block Assembly Diagrams*, place 1 white print B square atop 1 print A square, right sides facing. Stitch diagonally from corner to corner as shown. Trim ¼" beyond stitching. Press open to reveal triangle. Repeat for remaining corners to complete 1 block *(Block Diagram)*.

2. Make 80 blocks.

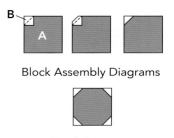

Block Assembly Diagrams

Block Diagram

Quit Assembly

1. Lay out blocks, white print sashing rectangles, and black and orange B squares as shown in *Quilt Top Assembly Diagram.*

2. Join into rows; join rows to complete quilt center.

3. Add black side inner borders to quilt center. Add black top and bottom inner borders to quilt.

4. Repeat for orange middle borders and white print outer borders.

Patterns are shown full size and are reversed for use with fusible web. Add ³⁄₁₆" seam allowance for hand appliqué.

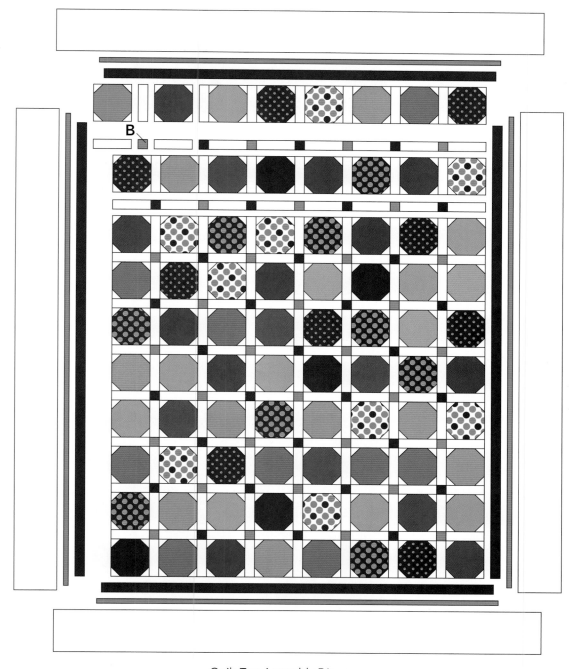

Quilt Top Assembly Diagram

Optional Appliqué

NOTE: Our appliqués are a Halloween witch and black cat. If desired, use another motif to coordinate with your blocks.

1. Position C squares and appliqué pieces atop outer border as shown in photo on page 77.
2. Appliqué in place by hand or machine.

Finishing

1. Divide backing into 2 (1⅝-yard) lengths. Join panels lengthwise. Seam will run horizontally.
2. Layer backing, batting, and quilt top; baste. Quilt as desired. Quilt shown was quilted with allover designs of pumpkins and spiderwebs *(Quilting Diagram)*.
3. Join 2¼"-wide black print strips into 1 continuous piece for straight-grain French-fold binding. Add binding to quilt.

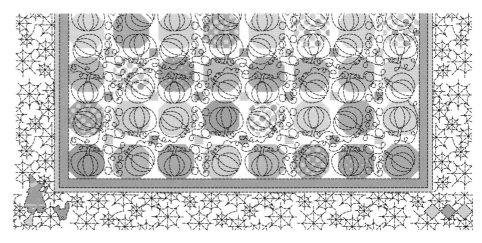

Quilting Diagram

DESIGNER

Florence Moy, a Human Resources professional, has been quilting for nearly twenty-five years. She enjoys designing quilts, trying out new quilt gadgets, and adding to her fabric stash while traveling. She also enjoys teaching quilt classes.

TRIED & TRUE

We fussy cut six squares from a large print from the Fantasia collection by Studio 8 for Exclusively Quilters to make a zippy placemat.

Lightning Strikes

Lightning never strikes twice in the same place. But you might make this striking twin-size quilt more than once. It goes together quickly, and is sure to delight a young musician.

PROJECT RATING: EASY

Size: 76" × 98"

MATERIALS

4¼ yards black print

1 fat quarter★ black print for border corners

2½ yards black stripe for border

1⅛ yards gold print for quilt and binding

½ yard each of 7 assorted prints in green, blue, white, black, and orange

6 yards backing fabric

Queen-size quilt batting

★fat quarter = 18" × 20"

Cutting

Measurements include ¼" seam allowances. Border strips are exact length needed. You may want to make them longer to allow for piecing variations.

From black print, cut:

- 5 (11¼"-wide) strips. From strips, cut 15 (11¼") squares. Cut squares in half diagonally in both directions to make 60 quarter-square B triangles.
- 1 (5⅞"-wide) strip. From strip, cut 4 (5⅞") squares. Cut squares in half diagonally to make 8 half-square A triangles.
- 3 (6½"-wide) **lengthwise** strips. From strips, cut 3 (6½" × 80½") sashing strips.
- 4 (2½"-wide) **lengthwise** strips. From strips, cut 2 (2½" × 80½") side inner borders and 2 (2½" × 62½") top and bottom inner borders.

From black print fat quarter, cut:

- 2 (7½"-wide) strips. From strips, cut 4 (7½") C squares.

From black stripe, cut:

- 4 (7½"-wide) **lengthwise** strips, centering stripe on each strip. From strips, cut 2 (7½" × 84½") side outer borders and 2 (7½" × 62½") top and bottom outer borders.

From gold print, cut:

- 2 (5⅞"-wide) strips. From strips, cut 8 (5⅞") squares. Cut squares in half diagonally to make 16 half-square A triangles.
- 10 (2¼"-wide) strips for binding.

From each assorted print, cut:

- 2 (5⅞"-wide) strips. From strips, cut 8 (5⅞") squares. Cut squares in half diagonally to make 16 half-square A triangles.

Lightning Row Assembly

1. Join 1 print A triangle and 1 black print A triangle as shown in *Triangle-Square Diagrams*. Make 8 triangle-squares.

Triangle-Square Diagrams

2. Join 1 black print B triangle and 2 print A triangles as shown in *Flying Geese Unit Diagrams*. Make 60 Flying Geese Units.

Flying Geese Diagrams

3. Referring to *Quilt Top Assembly Diagram*, join 8 Flying Geese Units to make 1 Row 1. Make 4 Row 1.

4. In a similar manner, make 4 Row 2 using 2 triangle-squares and 7 Flying Geese Units in each.

5. Join 1 Row 1 and 1 Row 2 to complete 1 Lightning Row. Make 4 Lightning rows.

Quilt Assembly

1. Lay out Lightning Rows and black print sashing strips as shown in *Quilt Top Assembly Diagram*. Join to complete quilt center.

2. Add black print side inner borders to quilt center. Add black print top and bottom inner borders to quilt.

3. Add black stripe side outer borders to quilt center.

Quilt Top Assembly Diagram

4. Add 1 black print C square to each end of black stripe top and bottom outer borders. Add borders to quilt.

Finishing

1. Divide backing into 2 (3-yard) lengths. Cut 1 piece in half lengthwise to make 2 narrow panels. Join 1 narrow panel to each side of wider panel; press seam allowances toward narrow panels.

2. Layer backing, batting, and quilt top; baste. Quilt as desired. Quilt shown was quilted with loopy meandering (*Quilting Diagram*).

3. Join 2¼"-wide gold print strips into 1 continuous piece for straight-grain French-fold binding. Add binding to quilt.

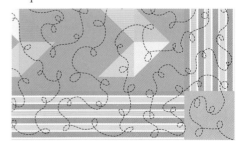

Quilting Diagram

TRIED & TRUE

We reversed the look of this design by using a light background.
Fabrics are from the Dandelion Daydream collection by Maywood Studio.

DESIGNER

Debbie Beaves is the designer and author at Violet Patch Quilts. She has been quilting and teaching for more than twenty-five years. Her ability to blend visually stunning designs with highly detailed and easy-to-follow patterns makes Debbie a favorite among her students. Designing fabrics and creating patterns for new collections keep her busy.

Victoria Star

Designer Lori Hein used a palette of soft taupe, blue, chocolate brown, and pistachio for this beautiful lap quilt.

PROJECT RATING: EASY

Size: 49" x 49"

MATERIALS

¾ yard light blue print

1 fat quarter* medium blue print

1⅛ yards dark green stripe

¾ yard light brown print

¾ yard light green print

1⅛ yards dark brown print

3 yards backing fabric

Twin-size quilt batting

*fat quarter = 18" × 20"

Cutting

Measurements include ¼" seam allowances. Border strips are exact length needed. You may want to make them longer to allow for piecing variations.

From light blue print, cut:
- 1 (8⅞"-wide) strip. From strip, cut 4 (8⅞") squares. Cut squares in half diagonally to make 8 half-square F triangles.
- 1 (4½"-wide) strip. From strip, cut 1 (4½") A square and 4 (4") C squares.
- 1 (2⅞"-wide) strip. From strip, cut 4 (2⅞") squares. Cut squares in half diagonally to make 8 half-square E triangles.
- 2 (2½"-wide) strips. From strips, cut 2 (2½" × 12½") J rectangles and 2 (2½" × 8½") I rectangles.

From medium blue print, cut:
- 1 (4½"-wide) strip. From strip, cut 4 (4½") A squares.

From dark green stripe, cut:
- 4 (4½"-wide) **lengthwise** strips, centering design on each. From strips, cut 4 (4½" × 35½") inner borders.

From light brown print, cut:
- 1 (3½"-wide) strip. From strip, cut 4 (3½") B squares.

- 6 (2½"-wide) strips. From strips, cut 2 (2½" × 16½") K rectangles, 2 (2½" × 12½") J rectangles, 8 (2½" × 10") H rectangles, and 8 (2½" × 6") G rectangles.

From light green print, cut:
- 1 (8⅞"-wide) strip. From strip, cut 4 (8⅞") squares. Cut squares in half diagonally to make 8 half-square F triangles.
- 1 (2⅞"-wide) strip. From strip, cut 4 (2⅞") squares. Cut squares in half diagonally to make 8 half-square E triangles.
- 1 (2½"-wide) strip. From strip, cut 4 (2½") D squares.
- 3 (1½"-wide) strips. From strips, cut 8 (1½" × 6") N rectangles and 8 (1½" × 4") M rectangles,

From dark brown print, cut:
- 5 (3½"-wide) strips. Piece strips to make 4 (3½" × 43½") outer borders.
- 6 (2¼"-wide) strips for binding.
- 2 (2"-wide) strips. From strips, cut 4 (2" × 16½") L rectangles.

Center Unit Assembly

1. Join 1 light blue print E triangle and 1 light green print E triangle to make a triangle-square *(Triangle-Square Diagrams)*. Make 8 small triangle-squares.

Triangle-Square Diagrams

2. In the same manner, make 8 large triangle-squares using light blue print and light green print F triangles.

3. Lay out light green print D squares, small triangle-squares, and 1 light blue print A square as shown in *Center Unit Assembly Diagrams*. Join into rows, join rows to complete center star.

4. Add light blue print I rectangles to top and bottom of center star; add light blue print J rectangles to sides of center star.

5. In the same manner, add light brown print J and K rectangles to complete Center Unit.

Quilt Assembly

1. Lay out 2 large triangle-squares and 1 dark brown print L rectangle as shown in *Side Unit Diagrams*. Join pieces to make 1 Side Unit. Make 4 Side Units.

2. Join 1 light blue print C square, 2 light green print M rectangles, 2 light green print N rectangles, 2 light brown print G rectangles, and 2 light brown print H rectangles as shown to make 1 Corner Unit *(Corner Unit Diagrams)*. Make 4 Corner Units.

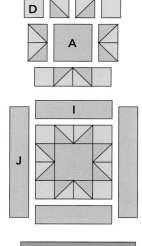

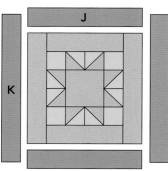

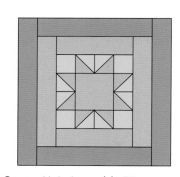

Center Unit Assembly Diagrams

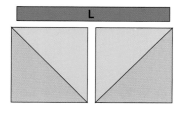

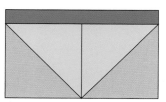

Side Unit Diagrams

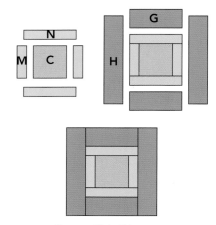

Corner Unit Diagrams

3. Lay out Center Unit, Side Units, and Corner Units as shown in *Quilt Top Assembly Diagram*. Join units to complete quilt center.

4. Add dark green stripe side inner borders to quilt center.

5. Join 1 medium blue print A square to each end of top and bottom inner borders. Add borders to quilt.

6. Add dark brown print side outer borders to quilt.

7. Join 1 light brown print B square to each end of top and bottom outer borders. Add borders to quilt.

Finishing

1. Divide backing into 2 (1½-yard) lengths. Cut 1 piece in half lengthwise to make 2 narrow panels. Join 1 narrow panel to wider panel. Remaining panel is extra and can be used to make a hanging sleeve.

2. Layer backing, batting, and quilt top; baste. Quilt as desired. Quilt shown was quilted with leaf designs *(Quilting Diagram)*.

3. Join 2¼"-wide dark brown print strips into 1 continuous piece for straight-grain French-fold binding. Add binding to quilt.

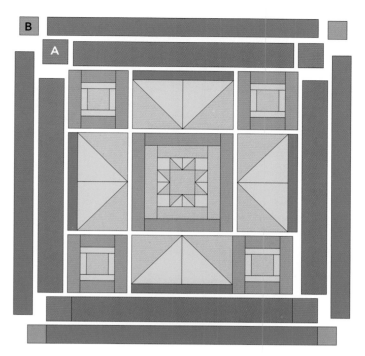

Quilt Top Assembly Diagram

Quilting Diagram

DESIGNER

Lori Hein was introduced to quilting in 1983, when she was a young mother of three living on her husband's family homestead near Spokane, Washington. She immediately loved working with the fabrics and block designs. When her children were nearly raised, Lori began working at a quilt shop, teaching classes, and designing her own quilt patterns. In 2005, she launched her Web site company, Cool Water Quilts.

Rainbow Hippie

This quilt is a dream to make in bright prints.
Easy piecing on paper foundations keeps strips straight.

PROJECT RATING: EASY

Size: 56" × 70"

Blocks: 20 (14") blocks

MATERIALS

½ yard black/green print (Fabric A)

1 yard dark pink print (Fabric B)

2¼ yards blue print for background
  and binding (Fabric C)

¼ yard light blue print (Fabric D)

⅜ yard light pink print (Fabric E)

½ yard yellow print (Fabric F)

1⅜ yards multi-color floral
  (Fabric G)

⅝ yard multi-color tie dye print
  (Fabric H)

⅜ yard black print (Fabric I)

¼ yard light green print (Fabric J)

300" of 15"-wide parchment paper
  or Golden Threads quilting paper

Glue stick

3½ yards backing fabric

Twin-size quilt batting

Cutting

Measurements include ¼" seam allowances. Stack rectangles and label them according to fabric and size as you cut them (example A-7").

From black/green print (A), cut:

• 2 (7"-wide) strips. From strips, cut 40 (7" × 1¾") rectangles.

From dark pink print (B), cut:

• 1 (9½"-wide) strip. From strip, cut 20 (9½" × 1¾") rectangles.

• 3 (7"-wide) strips. From strips, cut 60 (7" × 1¾") rectangles.

From blue print (C), cut:

• 1 (9½"-wide) strip. From strip, cut 20 (9½" × 1¾") rectangles.

• 5 (8½"-wide) strips. From strips, cut 20 (8½") squares. Cut squares in half diagonally to make 40 half-square triangles.

• 1 (7"-wide) strips. From strips, cut 20 (7" × 1¾") rectangles.

• 7 (2¼"-wide) strips for binding.

From light blue print (D), cut:

• 1 (6¼"-wide) strip. From strip, cut 20 (6¼" × 1¾") rectangles.

From light pink print (E), cut:

• 1 (5½"-wide) strip. From strip, cut 20 (5½" × 1¾") rectangles.

• 1 (3"-wide) strip. From strip, cut 20 (3" × 1¾") rectangles.

From yellow print (F), cut:

• 2 (7"-wide) strips. From strips, cut 40 (7" × 1¾") rectangles.

From multi-floral print (G), cut:

• 1 (15"-wide) strip. From strip, cut 20 (15" × 1¾") rectangles.

• 1 (9½"-wide) strip. From strip, cut 20 (9½" × 1¾") rectangles.

• 2 (7"-wide) strips. From strips, cut 40 (7" × 1¾") rectangles.

• 1 (5½"-wide) strip. From strip, cut 20 (5½" × 1¾") rectangles.

From multi-color tie dye print (H), cut:

• 1 (11"-wide) strip. From strip, cut 20 (11" × 1¾") rectangles.

• 1 (7"-wide) strip. From strip, cut 20 (7" × 1¾") rectangles.

From black print (I), cut:

• 1 (8"-wide) strip. From strip, cut 20 (8" × 1¾") rectangles.

From light green print (J), cut:
- 1 (5"-wide) strip. From strip, cut 20 (5" × 1¾") rectangles.

From paper, cut:
- 20 (14½") squares.

Block Assembly

NOTE: Make 20 each of Strips #1 through #8 as shown in *Strip Diagrams*. Stack strips and label them #1 through #8 as you make them.

1. Join 1 B-9½" rectangle and 1 G-15" rectangle to make 1 Strip #1.
2. Join 1 C-9½" rectangle, 1 J-5" rectangle, and 1 F-7" rectangle to make 1 Strip #2.
3. Join 1 H-7" rectangle, 1 G-5½" rectangle, and 1 A-7" rectangle to make 1 Strip #3.
4. Join 1 G-7" rectangle, 1 E-3" rectangle, and 1 B-7" rectangle to make 1 Strip #4.
5. Join 1 A-7" rectangle, 1 D-6¼" rectangle, and 1 H-11" rectangle to make 1 Strip #5.
6. Join 1 F-7" rectangle, 1 I-8" rectangle, and 1 G-7" rectangle to make 1 Strip #6.
7. Join 1 B-7" rectangle, 1 E-5½" rectangle, and 1 C-7" rectangle to make 1 Strip #7.
8. Join 1 G-9½" rectangle and 1 B-7" rectangle to make 1 Strip #8.
9. Draw a diagonal line from corner to corner on paper square as shown in *Paper Foundation Diagram*. Draw a second line ¼" away from the first line as shown.
10. Place 1 Strip #1 atop paper square, aligning edge of strip with second drawn line as shown in *Strip Placement Diagrams*. Hold in place with a few dabs of glue.

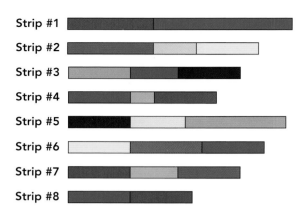

Strip Diagrams

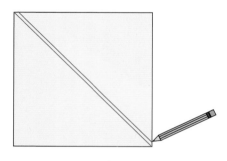

Paper Foundation Diagram

11. Place 1 Strip #2 atop Strip #1 right sides facing. Stitch strips together along bottom edge; open and press toward Strip #2.
12. In the same manner, add Strips #3 through #8.
13. Add 1 blue print triangle to Strip #4 and 1 blue print triangle to Strip #8 to complete piecing.
14. Turn foundation over, paper side up. Trim to 14½" square to complete 1 block, using edge of paper as a guide. Remove paper from block. Make 20 blocks.

Quilt Assembly

1. Lay out blocks as shown in *Quilt Top Assembly Diagram*.
2. Join into rows; join rows to complete quilt top.

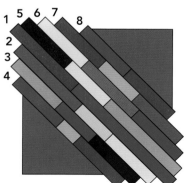

Strip Placement Diagrams

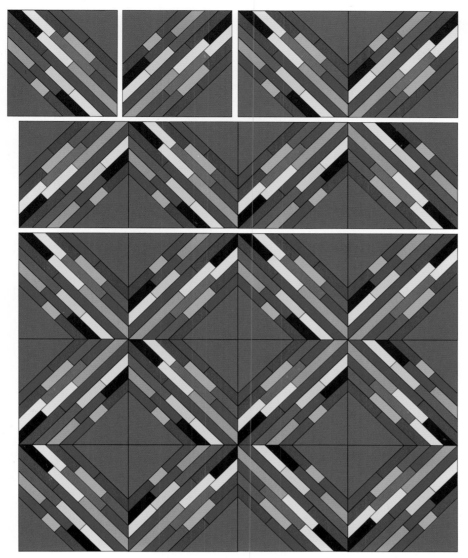

Quilt Top Assembly Diagram

Finishing

1. Divide backing into 2 (1¾-yard) lengths. Join panels lengthwise. Seam will run horizontally.

2. Layer backing, batting, and quilt top; baste. Quilt as desired. Quilt shown was quilted in the middle of each strip and with a peace sign in background (*Quilting Diagram*).

3. Join 2¼"-wide blue print strips into 1 continuous piece for straight-grain French-fold binding. Add binding to quilt.

Quilting Diagram

Sunflowers

Nature-theme prints provide a perfect background for appliquéd sunflowers.

PROJECT RATING: EASY

Size: 64½" × 73½"

MATERIALS

½ yard each of 12 assorted dark prints in red, blue, purple, and green for background

1 yard gold print for inner border and binding

1⅜ yards yellow print for sunflowers

½ yard brown print for sunflowers

1¼ yards gradated print for outer border

Paper-backed fusible web

4 yards backing fabric

Twin-size quilt batting

*fat quarter = 18" × 20"

Cutting

Measurements include ¼" seam allowances. Border strips are exact length needed. You may want to make them longer to allow for piecing variations. Patterns for Sunflower are on page 95. Follow manufacturer's instructions for using fusible web.

NOTE: Refer to photo on page 93 and *Quilt Top Assembly Diagram* on page 92 for color guidance for cutting squares and rectangles for background.

From assorted dark prints, cut a total of:

- 1 (9½" × 24½") A rectangle.
- 1 (9½" × 18½") B rectangle.
- 2 (9½" × 15½") C rectangles.
- 3 (9½" × 12½") D rectangles.
- 1 (15½") E square.
- 1 (12½" × 15½") F rectangle.
- 4 (12½") G squares.

- 2 (6½" × 18½") H rectangles.
- 2 (6½" × 12½") I rectangles.
- 1 (3½" × 12½") J rectangle.
- 5 (9½") K squares.
- 2 (6½" × 9½") L rectangles.
- 15 (6½") M squares.

From gold print, cut:

- 8 (2¼"-wide) strips for binding.
- 7 (1½"-wide) strips. Piece strips to make 2 (1½" × 63½") side inner borders and 2 (1½" × 56½") top and bottom inner borders.

From yellow print, cut:

- 17 Sunflowers.

From brown print, cut:

- 17 Centers.

From gradated print, cut:

- 8 (4¾"-wide) strips. Piece strips to make 2 (4¾" × 65½") side outer borders and 2 (4¾" × 65") top and bottom outer borders.

Quilt Assembly

1. Lay out squares and rectangles as shown in *Quilt Top Assembly Diagram* join into sections as shown.

2. Join sections to make 3 vertical rows. Join vertical rows to complete quilt center.

3. Add side inner borders to quilt center. Add top and bottom inner borders to quilt.

4. Repeat for outer borders.

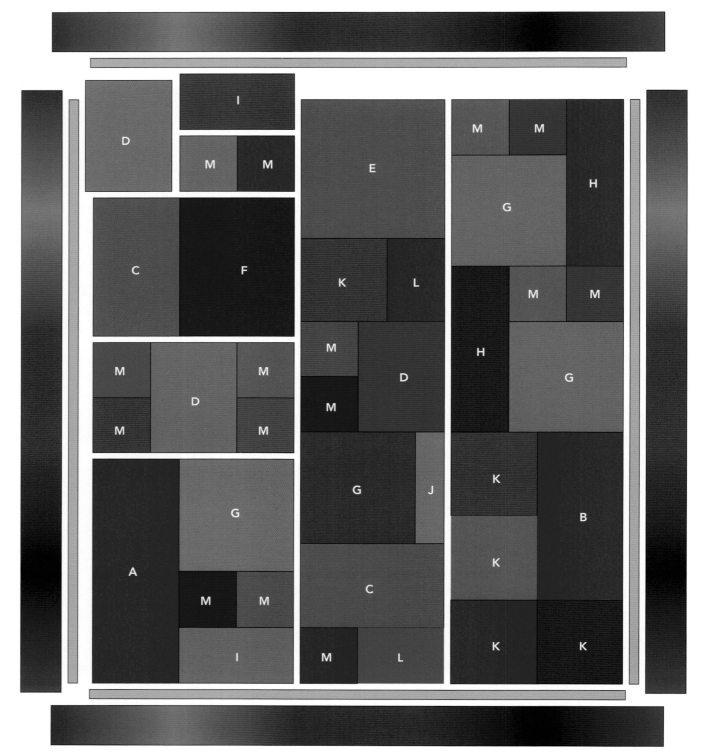

Quilt Top Assembly Diagram

Appliqué

1. Arrange Sunflowers and Centers on quilt as shown in photo. Fuse in place.

2. Machine appliqué Sunflower pieces using blanket stitch and brown thread.

Finishing

1. Divide backing into 2 (2-yard) lengths. Join panels lengthwise. Seam will run horizontally.

2. Layer backing, batting, and quilt top; baste. Quilt as desired. Quilt shown was quilted with an allover design *(Quilting Diagram)*.

3. Join 2¼"-wide gold print strips into 1 continuous piece for straight-grain French-fold binding. Add binding to quilt.

Quilting Diagram

DESIGNER

Michele Scott is an award-winning quilt artist who teaches, lectures, and designs fabric. Although she specializes in machine work and embellishments, Michele enjoys teaching a variety of classes.

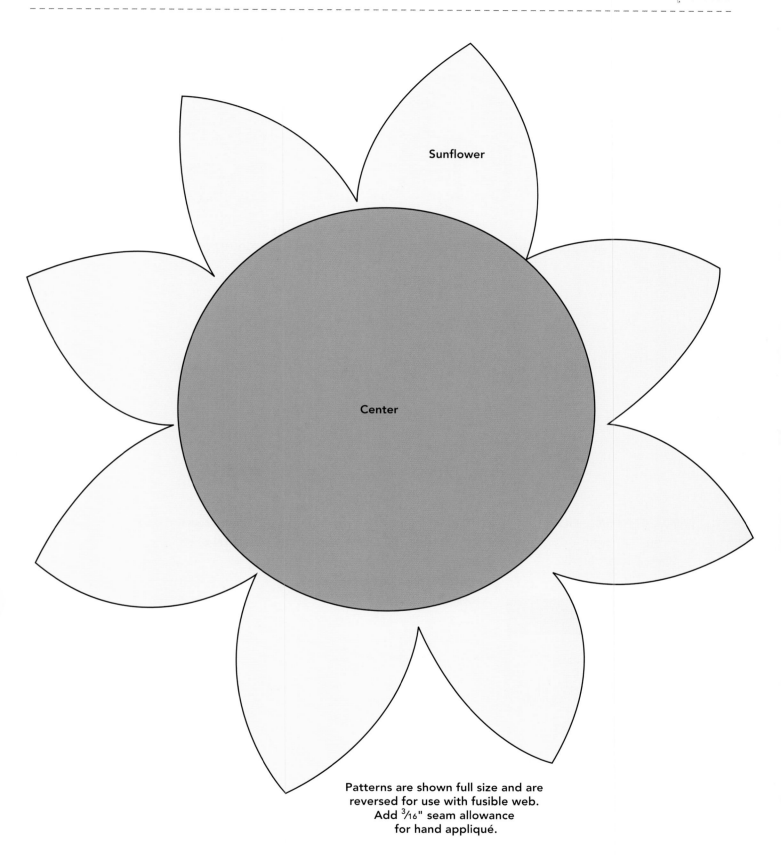

Sunflower

Center

Patterns are shown full size and are
reversed for use with fusible web.
Add ³⁄₁₆" seam allowance
for hand appliqué.

QUILT BY **Scott Hansen**.
MACHINE QUILTED BY **Becky Marshall**.

Split Pea Soup

Enjoy the freedom of casual piecing without matching seams!

PROJECT RATING: EASY

Size: 49" × 49"

Blocks: 49 (7") blocks

MATERIALS

16 fat quarters★ assorted light prints in yellow, orange, tan, and green

16 fat quarters★ assorted dark prints in brown, black, and green

3 yards backing fabric

Twin-size quilt batting

★fat quarter = 18" × 20"

Cutting

Measurements include ¼" seam allowances.

From assorted light prints, cut a total of:

- 16 (3"- to 4"-wide) strips in 8 matching pairs. From strips, cut 24 pairs of matching (5½"-long) D rectangles.
- 36 (1½"- to 2"-wide) strips in 12 matching sets of 3. From strips, cut 24 sets of 4 matching (5½"-long) C rectangles.
- 39 (1"-wide) strips in 13 matching sets of 3. From strips, cut 25 sets of 4 matching (1" × 5½") B rectangles.

From assorted dark prints, cut a total of :

- 18 (3"- to 4"-wide) strips in 9 matching pairs. From strips, cut 25 pairs of matching (5½"-long) D rectangles.
- 39 (1½"- to 2"-wide) strips in 13 matching sets of 3. From strips, cut 25 sets of 4 matching (5½"-long) C rectangles.
- 36 (1"-wide) strips in 12 matching sets of 3. From strips, cut 24 sets of 4 matching (1" × 5½") B rectangles.

From remainders of fat quarters, cut a total of:

- 13 (2¼"-wide) strips for binding.
- 34 (1½"-wide) strips. From each strip, cut 13 (1½") A squares.

Block Assembly

1. Lay out 9 assorted 1½" A squares as shown in *Nine Patch Unit Diagrams*. Join into rows; join rows to complete 1 Nine Patch Unit. Make 49 Nine Patch Units.

Nine Patch Unit Diagrams

2. Choose 1 set of 4 matching dark print B rectangles and 4 matching light print C rectangles and 2 matching light print D rectangles. Referring to *Sew Easy: Casual Piecing* on page 100, make 24 Block 1 *(Block 1 Diagram)*.

Block 1 Diagram

3. In the same manner, make 25 Block 2 using light B rectangles and dark C and D rectangles *(Block 2 Diagram)*.

Block 2 Diagram

Quilt Assembly

1. Lay out blocks as shown in *Quilt Top Assembly Diagram*.

2. Join blocks into rows; join rows to complete quilt top.

Quilt Top Assembly Diagram

Finishing

1. Divide backing into 2 (1½-yard) lengths. Cut 1 piece in half lengthwise to make 2 narrow panels. Join 1 narrow panel to wider panel. Remaining panel is extra and can be used to make a hanging sleeve.

2. Layer backing, batting, and quilt top; baste. Quilt as desired. Quilt shown was quilted with an allover swirl design *(Quilting Diagram)*.

3. Join 2¼"-wide assorted print strips into 1 continuous piece for straight-grain French-fold binding. Add binding to quilt.

Quilting Diagram

DESIGNER

Scott Hansen has been making quilts since he was fourteen years old. Now, in addition to working in retail management, he makes quilts for fabric companies and other artists from his design studio. Scott lives in Washington with his wife, three teenage children, eight chickens, four ducks, and two cats.

Casual Piecing

Use this quick and easy method to make asymmetrical blocks for *Split Pea Soup*.

1. Join 2 dark B rectangles and 3 light C rectangles as shown in *Photo A*. **NOTE:** Strip Set should measure at least 3½" high. From strip set, cut 2 (2½"-wide) #1 segments *(Photo B)*.

2. Trim segments to 3½" high *(Photo C)*. Segments do not have to be trimmed evenly. Sometimes the top will be trimmed more than the bottom. This will give the block a casual, random look.

3. Join 2 dark B rectangles, 1 light C rectangle, and 2 light D rectangles a shown in *Photo D*.
   NOTE: Strip Set should measure at least 7½" high. From strip set, cut 2 (2½"-wide) #2 segments.

4. Trim segments to 7½" high *(Photo E)*.

5. Lay out 1 Nine Patch Unit, 2 #1 segments, and 2 #2 s egments as shown in *Photo F*. Join into rows; join rows to complete 1 block *(Photo G)*.

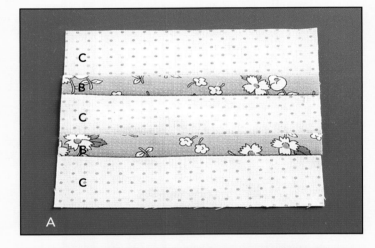

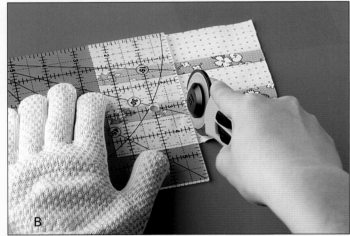

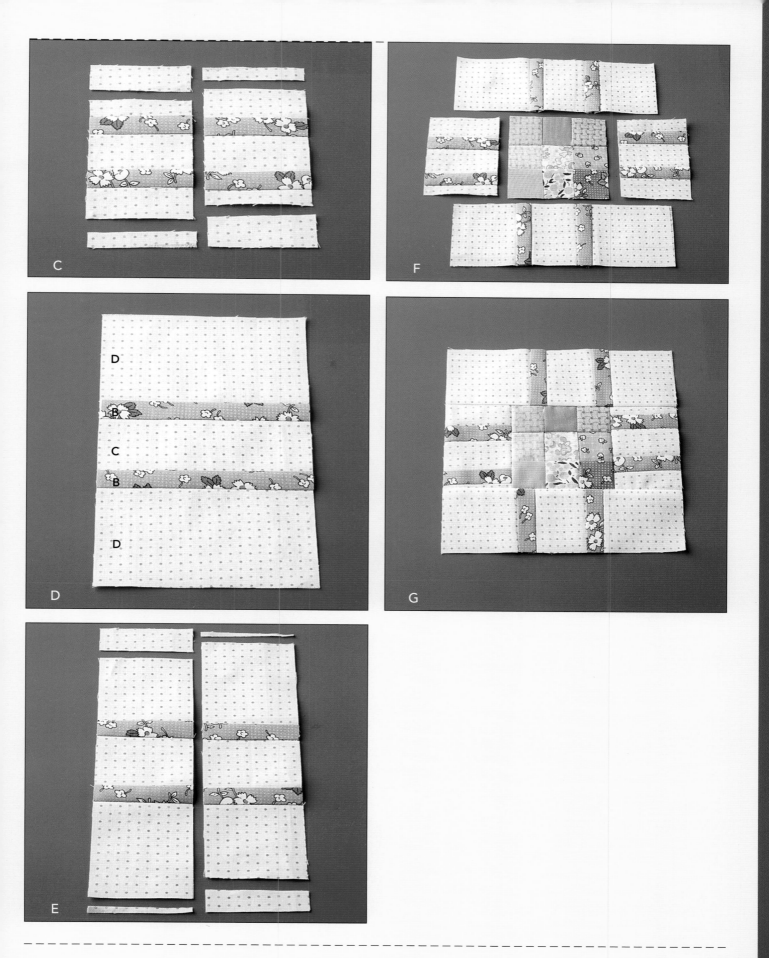

C

F

D

D
B
C
B
D

G

E

Spin City

Here's a modern twist using an appealing variety of 1930s reproduction prints.
This quilt brings new life to a traditional design. See *Sew Easy: Using Tri-Recs™ Tools*
on page 106 for an easy way to cut the pieces for this quilts

PROJECT RATING: EASY
Size: 50" × 58"
Blocks: 30 (8") blocks

MATERIALS

21 fat quarters★ assorted prints for
  blocks and pieced border
1⅝ yards white solid for blocks and
  inner border
½ yard brown print for binding
Tri-Recs™ Tools or template
  material
3¼ yards backing fabric
Twin-size quilt batting
★fat quarter = 18" × 20"

Cutting

Measurements include ¼" seam allowances. Border strips are exact length needed. You may want to make them longer to allow for piecing variations. Patterns for A and B triangles are on page 105.

> ### Sew **Smart**™
> Use the Tri-Recs™ Tools to make quick work of cutting A and B triangles.—Liz

From assorted fat quarters, cut a total of:
• 92 (4½" × 2½") C rectangles.
• 16 (2½") D squares.
• 30 sets of 4 matching A triangles.
From white solid, cut:
• 5 (1½"-wide) strips. Piece strips to make 2 (1½" × 48½") side inner borders and 2 (1½" × 42½") top and bottom inner borders.

• 10 (4½"-wide) strips. From strips, cut 120 B triangles and 120 B triangles reversed.

> ### Sew **Smart**™
> Stack strips with wrong sides facing to cut B and B reversed triangles at the same time.
> —Marianne

From brown print, cut:
• 6 (2¼"-wide) strips for binding.

Block Assembly

1. Join 1 print A triangle, 1 white B triangle, and 1 white B triangle reversed as shown in *Block Unit Diagrams*. Make 4 matching Block Units.

Block Unit Diagrams

2. Lay out Block Units as shown in *Block Assembly Diagram*. Join into rows; join rows to complete 1 block *(Block Diagram)*. Make 30 blocks.

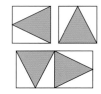

Block Assembly Diagram

Block Diagram

Border Assembly

1. Join 4 print D squares as shown in *Four Patch Unit Diagrams*. Make 4 Four Patch Units.

Four Patch Unit Diagrams

2. Referring to *Quilt Top Assembly Diagram*, join 25 C rectangles to make pieced side border. Make 2 pieced side borders.

3. In the same manner, make pieced top border using 21 C rectangles and 2 Four Patch Units.

4. Repeat for pieced bottom border.

Quilt Assembly

1. Lay out blocks as shown in *Quilt Top Assembly Diagram*.

2. Join blocks into rows; join rows to complete quilt center.

3. Add white side inner borders to quilt center. Add white top and bottom inner borders to quilt.

4. Repeat for pieced outer borders.

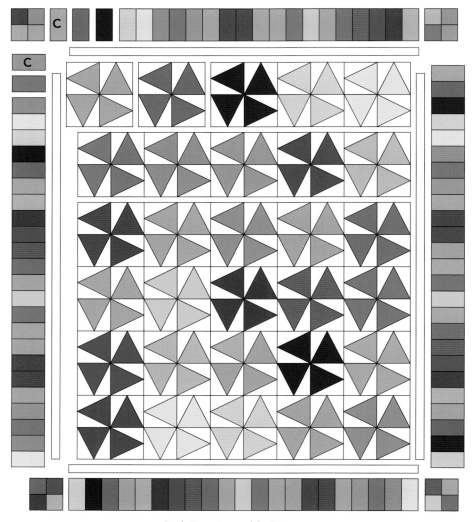

Quilt Top Assembly Diagram

Finishing

1. Divide backing into 2 (1⅝-yard) lengths. Join panels lengthwise. Seam will run horizontally.

2. Layer backing, batting, and quilt top; baste. Quilt as desired. Quilt shown was quilted with an allover swirl design *(Quilting Diagram)*.

3. Join 2¼"-wide brown print strips into 1 continuous piece for straight-grain French-fold binding. Add binding to quilt.

Quilting Diagram

DESIGNER

Designer Nancy Mahoney has been making quilts for more than twenty years. She enjoys combining traditional blocks and updated techniques to create dazzling quilts. Nancy has authored twelve books, all published by Martingale & Company. Her latest book is *Kaleidoscope Paper Piecing*.

TRIED & TRUE

This block is so versatile. We made scrappy blocks with a soft, dusty rose background in this new fabric collection by Whimsicals. It's called Simply Imagine from Red Rooster Fabrics.

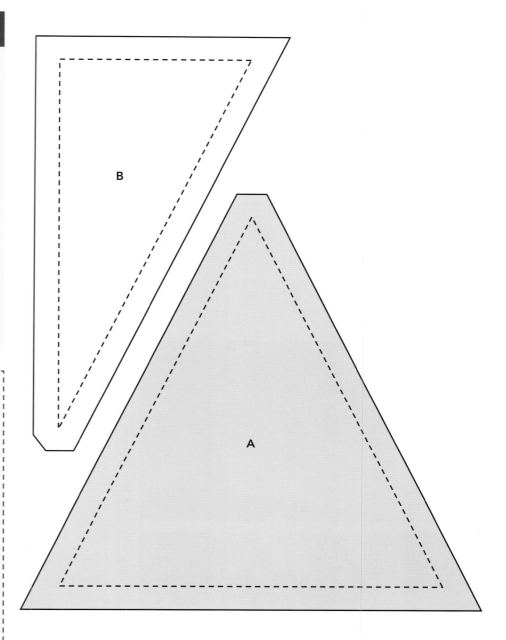

Sew Easy™

Using Tri-Recs™ Tools

Three-triangle units were nicknamed "Peaky and Spike" by quilter Doreen Speckmann, who used these units extensively in her quilts. The larger, central triangle is "Spike," and the smaller, side triangle is "Peaky." Follow our instructions for using the Tri-Recs™ tools to make cutting and piecing these units a snap.

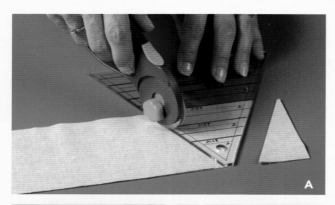

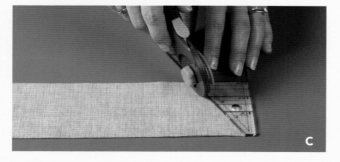

Cutting "Peaky and Spike" Triangles

1. Begin by cutting 1 fabric strip from each of the colors you wish to combine in a "Peaky and Spike" unit. To determine the strip size, add ½" to the desired finished size of the unit. For example, for a 4" finished unit, cut strips 4½" wide.

2. Working with the strip for the center "Spike" triangle, position the Tri tool atop the strip, aligning the mark corresponding to your strip width along bottom edge of strip. Cut along both angled sides of Tri tool *(Photo A)*.

3. Reposition Tri tool with strip width line along top edge of strip and side along previously cut edge. Cut another "Spike" triangle *(Photo B)*. Continue in this manner to cut desired number of "Spike" triangles.

4. Fold the strip for the side "Peaky" triangles in half with right sides together so you will be cutting two mirror image pieces at one time. Position the Recs tool atop the strip, aligning the mark corresponding to your strip width along bottom edge of strip. Cut on both sides of Recs tool to cut 2 "Peaky" triangles—1 right and 1 left *(Photo C)*.

5. Reposition Recs tool with strip width line along top edge of strip. Cut 2 more side "Peaky" triangles *(Photo D)*. Continue in this manner to cut desired number of pairs of "Peaky" triangles.

6. As you cut "Peaky" triangles, be sure to trim along the short angled line at the top of the Recs tool. This angled cut makes it easier to align pieces for sewing *(Photo E)*.

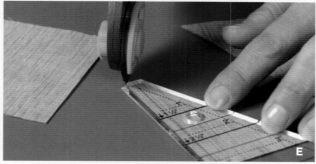

Assembling "Peaky and Spike" Units

1. Position right "Peaky" triangle along right side of "Spike" triangle, making sure the angle aligns with the side of the "Spike" triangle. Join pieces *(Photo F)*. Open out "Peaky" triangle; press seam allowances toward "Peaky" triangle.

2. Add left "Peaky" triangle to adjacent side as shown *(Photo G)*.

3. Open out "Peaky" triangle; press seam allowances toward "Peaky" triangle *(Photo H)*.

4. Trim points of seam allowances even with sides of "Peaky and Spike" unit *(Photo I)*.

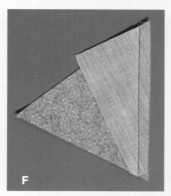

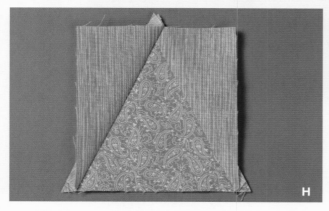

Phoebe

You can make this quilt in an afternoon.
It's perfect for a special baby on the way.

PROJECT RATING: EASY

Size: 37½" × 51½"

MATERIALS

1 yard large blue floral for blocks
¾ yard dark yellow print for sashing
1 yard blue stripe for sashing and
  binding
⅜ yard small blue floral for sashing
⅜ yard light yellow print for sashing
1⅝ yards backing fabric
Crib-size quilt batting

Cutting

Measurements include ¼" seam
allowances.

From large blue floral, cut:

• 5 (5"-wide) strips. From strips, cut 35
  (5") squares.

From dark yellow print, cut:

• 11 (1¾"-wide) strips for strip sets.

From blue stripe, cut:

• 5 (2½"-wide) strips for binding.
• 11 (1¾"-wide) strips for strip sets.

From small blue floral, cut:

• 5 (1¾"-wide) strips for strip sets.

From light yellow print, cut:

• 5 (1¾"-wide) strips for strip sets.

Sashing Assembly

1. Join 1 dark yellow print strip and 1
blue stripe strip as shown in *Strip Set
#1 Diagram*. Make 11 Strip Set #1.
From strip sets, cut 82 (5"-wide) #1
segments.

Strip Set #1 Diagram

2. In the same manner, join 1 light yellow
print strip and 1 small blue floral strip
as shown in *Strip Set #2 Diagram*.
Make 5 Strip Set #2. From strip sets,
cut 96 (1¾"-wide) #2 segments.

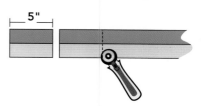

Strip Set #2 Diagram

3. Join 2 #2 segments as shown in
Sashing Square Diagrams. Make 48
Sashing Squares.

Sashing Square Diagrams

Quilt Assembly

1. Lay out large blue floral squares, #1 segments, and Sashing Squares as shown in *Quilt Top Assembly Diagram*.

2. Join into rows; join rows to complete quilt top.

Finishing

1. Layer backing, batting, and quilt top; baste. Quilt as desired. Quilt shown was quilted in the ditch *(Quilting Diagram)*.

2. Join 2½"-wide blue stripe strips into 1 continuous piece for straight-grain French-fold binding. Add binding to quilt.

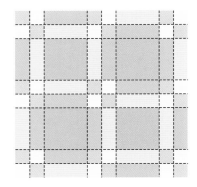

Quilting Diagram

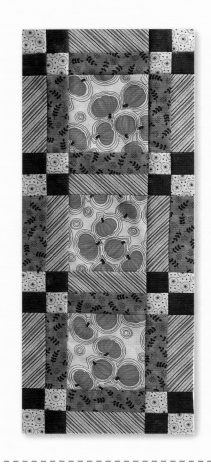

Quilt Top Assembly Diagram

SIZE OPTIONS

	Throw (58½" × 72½")	Twin (65½" × 86½")	Table Runner (9½" × 23½")
Large Blue Floral Squares	80	108	3
Strip Set #1 Segments	178	237	10
Strip Set #2 Segments	198	260	16

MATERIALS

	Throw	Twin	Table Runner
Large Blue Floral	1½ yards	2⅛ yards	1 fat eighth★
Yellow Print	1¼ yards	1⅝ yards	1 fat eighth★
Blue Stripe	1¾ yards	2⅛ yards	1 fat eighth★
Small Blue Floral	⅝ yard	¾ yard	1 fat eighth★
Pale Yellow Print	⅝ yard	¾ yard	1 fat eighth★
Backing Fabric	3½ yards	5¼ yards	⅜ yard
Batting	Twin-size	Twin-size	Craft-size

★fat eighth = 9" × 20"

Web **Extra**

Go to FonsandPorter.com/phoebesizes to download *Quilt Top Assembly Diagrams* **for these size options.**

Color Wave

Play with color as you make this contemporary wallhanging for your home or office. Nancy Mahoney's inspiration for her quilt was a display created by David Sweet, design director for P&B Textiles, to showcase the company's collection of tonal textured fabrics.

PROJECT RATING: EASY

Size: 48" × 39"

MATERIALS

1¾ yards black print for background and binding

47 fat eighths★ assorted prints in pink, lavender, purple, blue, teal, green, yellow, brown, and red

Paper-backed fusible web

1½ yards backing fabric

Crib-size quilt batting

★fat eighth = 9" × 20"

Cutting

Measurements include ¼" seam allowances. Patterns for Circles are on page 114. Refer to photo for color placement of Circles. Follow manufacturer's instructions for using fusible web. Refer to *Sew Easy: Windowing Fusible Appliqué* on page 115.

From black print, cut:

- 1 (48½" × 39½") background rectangle.
- 5 (2¼"-wide) strips for binding.

From assorted print fat eighths, cut a total of:

- 7 (6") A Circles.
- 6 (5½") B Circles.
- 13 (4½") C Circles.
- 23 (4") D Circles.
- 12 (3½") E Circles.
- 18 (3") F Circles.
- 38 (2½") G Circles.

Quilt Assembly

1. Referring to photo on page 113, fuse circles to black print background rectangle.

> ### Sew **Smart**™
>
> **Work on an appliqué pressing sheet when fusing so you don't get fusible residue on your ironing surface. —Marianne**

2. Trim circles even with edges of background rectangle.

3. Layer backing, batting, and quilt top; baste. Quilt as desired. Quilt shown was quilted with a spiral design, using matching thread in each circle, and with an allover swirl design using black thread in background *(Quilting Diagram)*.

4. Join 2¼"-wide black print strips into 1 continuous piece for straight-grain French-fold binding. Add binding to quilt. ✳

Quilting Diagram

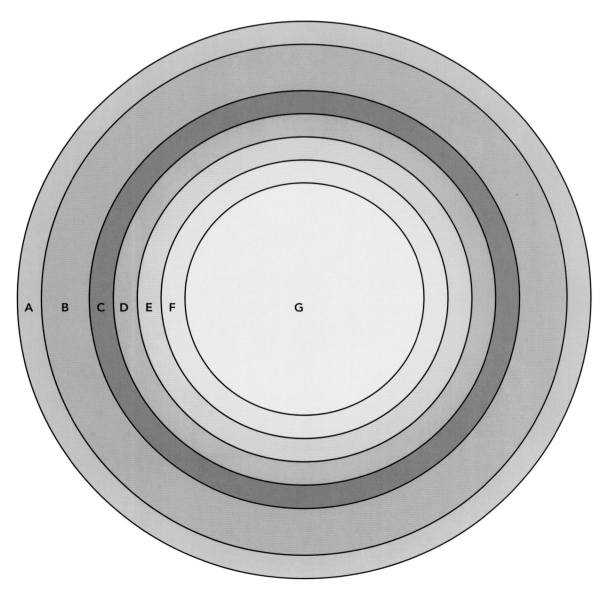

Windowing Fusible Appliqué

Choose a lightweight "sewable" fusible product. The staff at your favorite quilt shop can recommend brands. Always read and follow manufacturer's instructions for proper fusing time and iron temperature.

1. Trace appliqué motifs onto paper side of fusible web, making a separate tracing for each appliqué needed (*Photo A*).

A

2. Roughtly cut out drawn appliqué shapes, cutting about ¼" outside drawn lines (*Photo B*).

B

3. "Window" fusible by trimming out the interior of the shape, leaving a scant ¼" inside drawn line (*Photo C*). Follow manufacturer's instructions to fuse web side of each shape to wrong side of appliqué fabric.

C

4. Cut out appliqués, cutting carefully on drawn outline (*Photo D*). Only a thin band of fusible web frames the shape.

D

5. Peel off paper backing (*Photo E*). Position appliqué in place on background fabric, and follow manufacturer's instructions to fuse shapes in place.

E

Sew **Smart**™
If you have trouble peeling off the paper backing, try scoring paper with a pin to give you an edge to begin with. —Marianne

Sunset Runner

This table runner with neutral organic bordering a burst of color in the center would feel at home in any style decor.

PROJECT RATING: EASY

Size: 16" × 40"

MATERIALS

20 (2½"-wide) strips assorted batiks in red, purple, yellow, and orange (or 1 Jelly Roll™★)

5 (2½"-wide) strips assorted green batiks for appliqué pieces and binding

20 (5") squares of assorted beige and tan batiks (or 1 Charm Pack™★★)

Paper-backed fusible web

½ yard backing fabric

Craft-size quilt batting

★Jelly Roll™ = 40 (2½" × 45") strips

★★Charm Pack™ = 42 (5") squares

Cutting

Measurements include ¼" seam allowances. Appliqué patterns are on page 119.

From assorted red, purple, orange, and yellow strips, cut:

• 20 (2½" × 8½") rectangles.

From assorted green strips, cut:

• 2 Stems.

• 14 Leaves.

> ### Sew Smart™
> Purchase precut pieces to make your piecing faster.

From assorted squares, cut:

• 20 (4½") squares.

Table Runner Assembly

1. Join assorted rectangles as shown in *Center Diagram*.

Center Diagram

2. Join 10 assorted squares as shown in *Border Diagram*. Make 2 Borders.

Border Diagram

3. Add Borders to Center as shown in *Table Runner Assembly Diagram*.

4. Referring to photo, arrange Stems and Leaves atop table runner; fuse in place. Machine-appliqué using green thread and blanket stitch.

Finishing

1. Layer backing, batting, and quilt top; baste. Quilt as desired. Quilt shown was quilted around appliqué pieces, with an allover curvy design in center and allover mosaic design in border background *(Quilting Diagram)*.

2. Join remainders of 2½"-wide green strips into 1 continuous piece for straight-grain French-fold binding. Add binding to quilt.

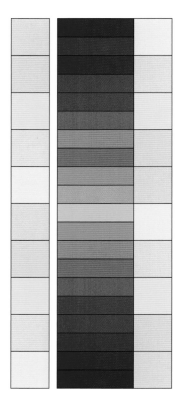

Table Runner Assembly Diagram

Quilting Diagram

DESIGNER

Edyta credits her family for her love of quilting and constant inspiration. As a designer for Moda, she shares her fabrics, quilts, and experiences with enthusiastic audiences worldwide. See more of Edyta's wonderful quilts in her book *Friendship Triangles*, published by Landauer Publishing.

TRIED & TRUE

To suit your decor, change the center's colors, such as this blue and green combination, made with the other half of the Jelly Roll™ used in the featured project, from the Over the Rainbow batik collection by Laundry Basket Quilts for Moda Fabrics.

Stem

Leaf

Shooting Stars
Table Runner

This table runner is so quick and easy,
you'll want to make two—one for yourself and one for a friend.

PROJECT RATING: EASY
Size: 19" × 55"
Blocks:
1 (12") Shooting Star block
8 (6") Friendship Star blocks

MATERIALS

¾ yard tan print for background
⅜ yard green print for outer border
⅝ yard rust stripe for inner border
and binding
4 fat quarters★ assorted prints in
brown, green, gold, and rust
⅞ yard backing fabric
Crib-size quilt batting
★fat quarter = 18" × 20"

Cutting

Measurements include ¼" seam allowances. Border strips are exact length needed. You may want to make them longer to allow for piecing variations.

From tan print, cut:
- 1 (5¼"-wide) strip. From strip, cut 1 (5¼") square. Cut square in half diagonally in both directions to make 4 quarter-square E triangles.
- 2 (3½"-wide) strips. From strips, cut 8 (3½" × 6½") G rectangles.
- 2 (2⅞"-wide) strips. From strips, cut 18 (2⅞") squares. Cut squares in half diagonally to make 36 half-square A triangles.
- 3 (2½"-wide) strips. From strips, cut 40 (2½") B squares.

From green print, cut:
- 3 (3"-wide) strips. From strips, cut 2 (3" × 35½") I rectangles and 2 (3" × 9½") H rectangles.

From rust stripe, cut:
- 5 (2¼"-wide) strips for binding.
- 4 (1½"-wide) strips. From 1 strip, cut 2 (1½" × 14½") top and bottom inner borders. Piece remaining strips to make 2 (1½" × 48½") side inner borders.

From brown print fat quarter, cut:
- 1 (4⅞"-wide) strip. From strip, cut 2 (4⅞") squares. Cut squares in half diagonally to make 4 half-square F triangles.
- 1 (3"-wide) strip. From strip, cut 6 (3") J squares.
- 1 (2⅞"-wide) strip. From strip, cut 4 (2⅞") squares. Cut squares in half diagonally to make 8 half-square A triangles.
- 1 (2½"-wide) strip. From strip, cut 2 (2½") B squares.

From green print fat quarter, cut:
- 1 (5¼"-wide) strip. From strip, cut 1 (5¼") square. Cut square in half diagonally in both directions to make 4 quarter-square E triangles.
- 1 (3"-wide) strip. From strip, cut 6 (3") J squares.
- 1 (2⅞"-wide) strip. From strip, cut 4 (2⅞") squares. Cut squares in half diagonally to make 8 half-square A triangles.
- 1 (2½"-wide) strip. From strip, cut 2 (2½") B squares.

From gold print fat quarter, cut:
- 1 (4½"-wide) strip. From strip, cut 1 (4½") C square and 4 (4½" × 2½") D rectangles.
- 1 (3"-wide) strip. From strip, cut 4 (3") J squares.
- 1 (2⅞"-wide) strip. From strip, cut 4 (2⅞") squares. Cut squares in half diagonally to make 8 half-square A triangles.
- 1 (2½"-wide) strip. From strip, cut 2 (2½") B squares.

From rust print fat quarter, cut:
- 1 (3"-wide) strip. From strip, cut 4 (3") J squares.
- 1 (2⅞"-wide) strip. From strip, cut 6 (2⅞") squares. Cut squares in half diagonally to make 12 half-square A triangles.
- 1 (2½"-wide) strip. From strip, cut 2 (2½") B squares.

Friendship Star Block Assembly

1. Join 1 tan print A triangle and 1 green print A triangle to make a triangle-square (*Triangle-Square Diagrams*). Make 8 green triangle squares.

Triangle-Square Diagrams

2. In the same manner, make 8 brown triangle-squares, 8 gold triangle-squares, and 12 rust triangle-squares.

3. Lay out 4 matching triangle-squares, 1 print B square, and 4 tan print B squares as shown in *Friendship Star Block Assembly Diagram*. Join into rows; join rows to complete 1 Friendship Star block (*Friendship Star Block Diagram*). Make 8 Friendship Star blocks.

Friendship Star Block Assembly Diagram

Friendship Star Block Diagram

Shooting Star Block Assembly

1. Referring to *Diagonal Seams Diagrams*, place 1 tan print B square atop 1 gold print D rectangle, right sides facing. Stitch diagonally from corner to corner as shown. Trim ¼" beyond stitching. Press open to reveal triangle to complete 1 Diagonal Seams Unit. Make 4 Diagonal Seams Units.

Diagonal Seams Diagrams

2. Lay out 1 Diagonal Seams Unit, 1 rust triangle-square, and 1 tan print B square as shown in *Corner Unit Diagrams*. Join to complete 1 Corner Unit. Make 4 Corner Units.

Corner Unit Diagrams

3. Lay out 1 brown print F triangle, 1 green print E triangle, and 1 tan print E triangle as shown in *Side Unit Diagram*. Join triangles to complete 1 Side Unit. Make 4 Side Units.

Side Unit Diagrams

4. Lay out 4 Corner Units, 4 Side Units, and 1 gold print C square as shown in *Shooting Star Block Assembly Diagram*. Join into rows; join rows to complete Shooting Star block (*Shooting Star Block Diagram*).

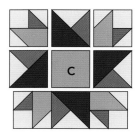

Shooting Star Block Assembly Diagram

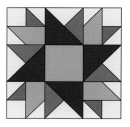

Shooting Star Block Diagram

Table Runner Assembly

1. Lay out blocks and tan print G rectangles as shown in *Assembly Diagram*. Join into rows; join rows to complete table runner center.

2. Add rust print side inner borders to table runner center. Add rust print top and bottom inner borders to table runner.

3. Lay out 6 assorted print J squares and 1 green print I rectangle as shown in *Assembly Diagram* on page 123. Join to make 1 side outer border. Make 2 side outer borders.

4. In the same manner, join 4 assorted print J squares and 1 green print H rectangle to make top border. Repeat for bottom border.

5. Add side pieced outer borders to table runner center. Add top and bottom pieced borders to table runner.

Quilting Diagram

Assembly Diagram

TRIED & TRUE

We used country prints from the Rise 'N Shine collection by Glenna Hailey and Maywood Studio for a fresh look.

DESIGNER

Gudrun Erla was born and raised in Iceland, and moved to Minnesota in 2003. She has published over 45 patterns and six books, and has designed several fabric collections for Red Rooster Fabrics.

Finishing

1. Cut backing piece in half lengthwise to make 2 narrow panels. Join panels along short edges.

2. Layer backing, batting, and quilt top; baste. Quilt as desired. Quilt shown was quilted with petal and feather designs in the Shooting Star block, with an allover swirl design in the center background, and in the ditch around inner border *(Quilting Diagram)*.

3. Join 2¼"-wide rust stripe strips into 1 continuous piece for straight-grain French-fold binding. Add binding to quilt.

Sunny Trio

Patrick Lose's whimsical style shines through in this sunny wallhanging.
It would also work well as a table runner.

PROJECT RATING: EASY

Size: 12" × 32"

Blocks: 3 (8") blocks

MATERIALS

½ yard turquoise print for blocks and binding

¼ yard purple print for sashing and border

1 fat quarter★ gold print for blocks

1 fat eighth★★ brown print for blocks

1 fat quarter★ green print for blocks

Paper-backed fusible web

½ yard backing fabric

Craft-size quilt batting

★fat quarter = 18" × 20"

★★fat eighth = 9" × 20"

Cutting

Measurements include ¼" seam allowances. Border strips are exact length needed. You may want to make them longer to allow for piecing variations. Patterns for appliqué are on page 127. Follow manufacturer's instructions for using fusible web.

From turquoise print, cut:

- 1 (8½"-wide) strip. From strip, cut 3 (8½") squares.
- 3 (2¼"-wide) strips for binding.

From purple print, cut:

- 3 (2½"-wide) strips. From strips, cut 2 (2½" × 32½") side borders and 4 (2½" × 8½") sashing rectangles.

From gold print, cut:

- 3 Flowers.

From brown print, cut:

- 3 Flower Centers.

From green print, cut:

- 9 Leaves.

Block Assembly

1. Referring to *Block Diagram*, arrange 1 Flower, 1 Flower Center, and 3 Leaves on 1 turquoise background square as shown. Trim excess leaves under flower and even with edges of background square. Fuse pieces in place.

Sew **Smart**™

Work on an appliqué pressing sheet when fusing so you don't get fusible residue on your ironing surface. —Liz

Block Diagram

2. Machine appliqué using matching thread and satin stitch. Satin stitch leaf veins as shown to complete 1 block *(Block Diagram)*. Make 3 blocks.

Quilt Assembly

1. Lay out blocks and purple print sashing rectangles as shown in *Quilt Top Assembly Diagram.* Join to complete quilt center.

2. Add purple print side borders to quilt center.

Finishing

1. Layer backing, batting, and quilt top; baste. Quilt as desired. Quilt shown was echo quilted in blocks and with wavy parallel lines in sashing and borders *(Quilting Diagram)*. The quilting thread colors match the fabrics.

2. Join 2¼"-wide turquoise print strips into 1 continuous piece for straight-grain French-fold binding. Add binding to quilt.

DESIGNER

Patrick Lose has been an artist and illustrator since childhood, and has spent his professional years in a variety of creative fields—quilts, wearable art, stationery products, and home décor. He is well known for his many fabric collections. Patrick is an author of quilting and crafting books, and has appeared on several television programs.

Quilt Top Assembly Diagram

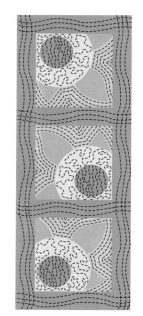

Quilting Assembly Diagram

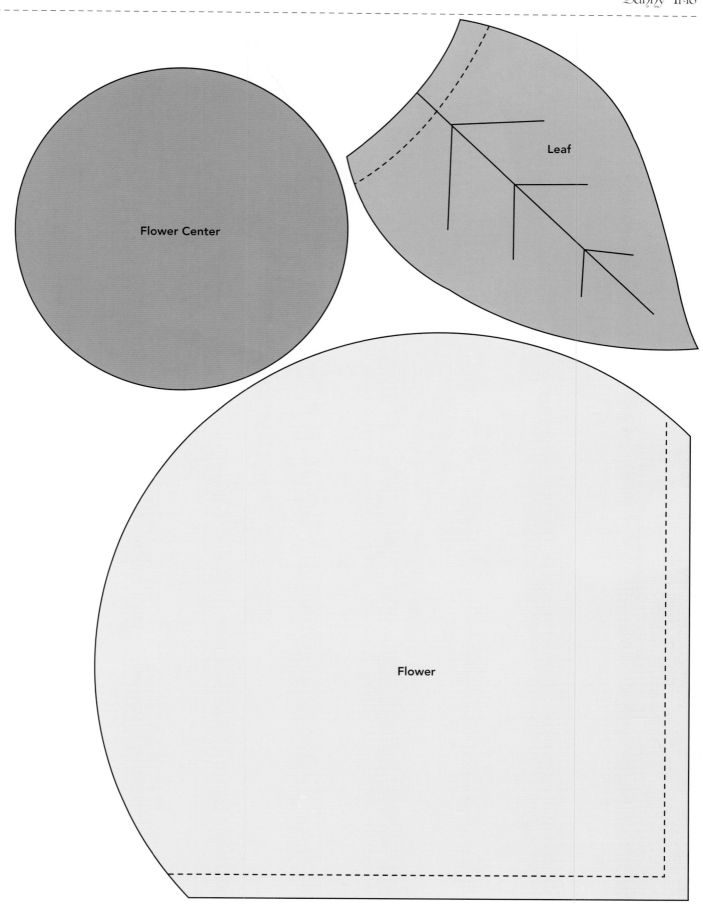

Flower Center

Leaf

Flower

Stars of the Past

These easy-to-piece star blocks are a quick way to show off a great collection of fabric. The stars have three-dimensional folded fabric points!

PROJECT RATING: EASY

Size: 49" × 69"

Blocks: 24 (10") blocks

MATERIALS

36 (10") squares in assorted white, red, blue, and yellow prints or 1 Layer Cake★

1 yard blue print for border

1¼ yards blue solid for blocks and binding

¾ yard red stripe for blocks

3¼ yards backing fabric

Twin-size quilt batting

★Layer Cake = 42 (10") squares

Cutting

Measurements include ¼" seam allowances. Border strips are exact length needed. You may want to make them longer to allow for piecing variations.

From each of 24 (10") squares, cut as shown in *Cutting Diagram*:

- 1 (4") A square.
- 4 (4" × 2¾") B rectangles.
- 4 (2¾") C squares. *(Cutting Diagram)*

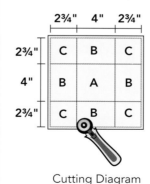

Cutting Diagram

From each of 12 (10") squares, cut:

- 16 (2¼") D squares.

From blue print, cut:

- 6 (5"-wide) strips. Piece strips to make 2 (5" × 60½") side borders and 2 (5" × 49½") top and bottom borders.

From blue solid, cut:

- 7 (2¼"-wide) strips for binding.
- 14 (1½"-wide) strips. From strips, cut 24 (1½" × 10½") F rectangles and 24 (1½" × 8½") E rectangles.

From red stripe, cut:

- 14 (1½"-wide) strips. From strips, cut 24 (1½" × 10½") F rectangles and 24 (1½" × 8½") E rectangles.

Block Assembly

1. Choose 4 matching B rectangles and 4 C squares, 8 matching D squares, and 1 A square.

2. Fold D squares in half diagonally, wrong sides facing. Press to make star points.

3. Referring to *Star Point Unit Diagrams,* place 1 star point atop 1 B rectangle, aligning raw edges as shown. Repeat for opposite end of rectangle; baste star points to rectangle. Make 4 Star Point Units.

Star Point Unit Diagrams

4. Lay out Star Point Units, A square, and C squares as shown in *Block Assembly Diagrams.* Join to make block center. Make 24 Block Centers.

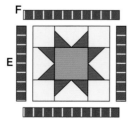

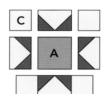

Block Assembly Diagrams

5. Add 2 red stripe E rectangles and 2 red stripe F rectangles to 1 block center to complete 1 red block *(Block Diagrams).* Make 12 red blocks.

6. In the same manner, make 12 blue blocks using blue solid E and F rectangles.

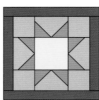

MAKE 12

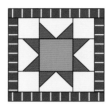

MAKE 12

Block Diagrams

Quilt Assembly

1. Lay out blocks as shown in *Quilt Top Assembly Diagram.* Join into rows; join rows to complete quilt center.

2. Add blue print side borders to quilt center. Add top and bottom borders to quilt.

Finishing

1. Divide backing into 2 (1⅝-yard) lengths. Join panels lengthwise. Seam will run horizontally.

Quilt Top Assembly Diagram

2. Layer backing, batting, and quilt top; baste. Quilt as desired. Quilt shown was outline quilted around stars, with an egg and dart variation in block borders, and overall meandering with stars in border *(Quilting Diagram)*.

3. Join 2¼"-wide blue strips into 1 continuous piece for straight-grain French-fold binding. Add binding to quilt.

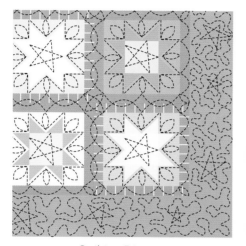

Quilting Diagram

DESIGNER

Bev Getschel fell in love with quilting in 2003, after having sewn all her life. She is the winner of several awards, and her work is regularly published in quilting magazines.

General Instructions

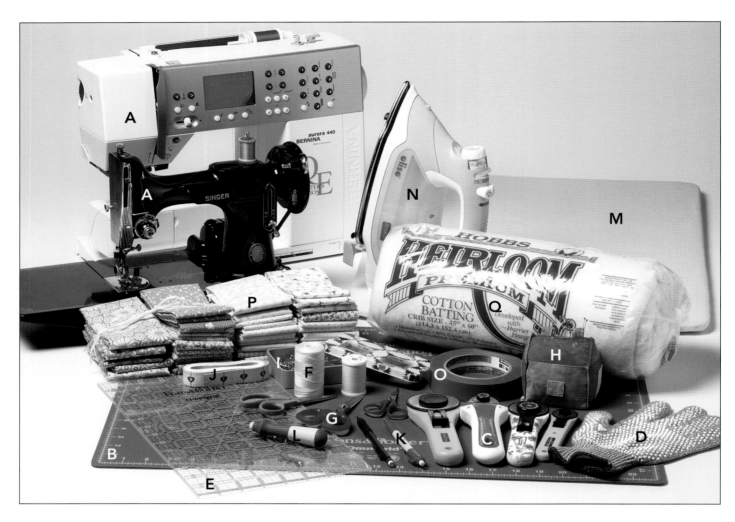

Basic Supplies

You'll need a **sewing machine (A)** in good working order to construct patchwork blocks, join blocks together, add borders, and machine quilt. We encourage you to purchase a machine from a local dealer, who can help you with service in the future, rather than from a discount store. Another option may be to borrow a machine from a friend or family member. If the machine has not been used in a while, have it serviced by a local dealer to make sure it is in good working order. If you need an extension cord, one with a surge protector is a good idea.

A **rotary cutting mat (B)** is essential for accurate and safe rotary cutting. Purchase one that is no smaller than 18" × 24".

Rotary cutting mats are made of "self-healing" material that can be used over and over.

A **rotary cutter (C)** is a cutting tool that looks like a pizza cutter, and has a very sharp blade. We recommend starting with a standard size 45mm rotary cutter. Always lock or close your cutter when it is not in use, and keep it out of the reach of children.

A **safety glove** (also known as a *Klutz Glove*) **(D)** is also recommended. Wear your safety glove on the hand that is holding the ruler in place. Because it is made of cut-resistant material, the safety glove protects your non-cutting hand from accidents that can occur if your cutting hand slips while cutting.

An acrylic **ruler (E)** is used in combination with your cutting mat and rotary cutter. We recommend the Fons & Porter

8" × 14" ruler, but a 6" × 12" ruler is another good option. You'll need a ruler with inch, quarter-inch, and eighth-inch markings that show clearly for ease of measuring. Choose a ruler with 45-degree-angle, 30-degree-angle, and 60-degree-angle lines marked on it as well.

Since you will be using 100% cotton fabric for your quilts, use **cotton or cotton-covered polyester thread (F)** for piecing and quilting. Avoid 100% polyester thread, as it tends to snarl.

Keep a pair of small **scissors (G)** near your sewing machine for cutting threads.

Thin, good quality **straight pins (H)** are preferred by quilters. The pins included with pin cushions are normally too thick to use for piecing, so discard them. Purchase a box of nickel-plated brass **safety pins** size #1 **(I)** to use for pin-basting the layers of your quilt together for machine quilting.

Invest in a 120"-long dressmaker's **measuring tape (J)**. This will come in handy when making borders for your quilt.

A 0.7–0.9mm mechanical **pencil (K)** works well for marking on your fabric.

Invest in a quality sharp **seam ripper (L)**. Every quilter gets well-acquainted with her seam ripper!

Set up an **ironing board (M)** and **iron (N)** in your sewing area. Pressing yardage before cutting, and pressing patchwork seams as you go are both essential for quality quiltmaking. Select an iron that has steam capability.

Masking **tape (O)** or painter's tape works well to mark your sewing machine so you can sew an accurate ¼" seam. You will also use tape to hold your backing fabric taut as you prepare your quilt sandwich for machine quilting.

The most exciting item that you will need for quilting is **fabric (P)**. Quilters generally prefer 100% cotton fabrics for their quilts. This fabric is woven from cotton threads, and has a lengthwise and a crosswise grain. The term "bias" is used to describe the diagonal grain of the fabric. If you make a 45-degree angle cut through a square of cotton fabric, the cut edges will be bias edges, which are quite stretchy. As you learn more quiltmaking techniques, you'll learn how bias can work to your advantage or disadvantage.

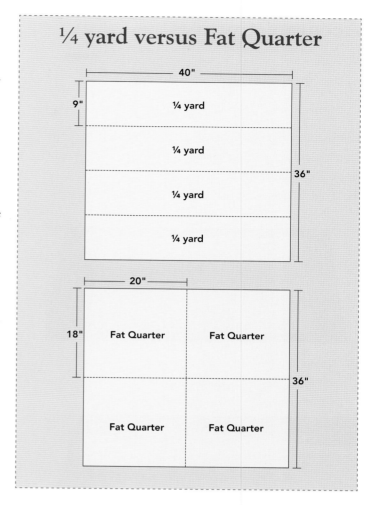

Fabric is sold by the yard at quilt shops and fabric stores. Quilting fabric is generally about 40"–44" wide, so a yard is about 40" wide by 36" long. As you collect fabrics to build your own personal stash, you will buy yards, half yards (about 18" × 40"), quarter yards (about 9" × 40"), as well as other lengths.

Many quilt shops sell "fat quarters," a special cut favored by quilters. A fat quarter is created by cutting a half yard down the fold line into two 18" × 20" pieces (fat quarters) that are sold separately. Quilters like the nearly square shape of the fat quarter because it is more useful than the narrow regular quarter yard cut.

Batting (Q) is the filler between quilt top and backing that makes your quilt a quilt. It can be cotton, polyester, cotton-polyester blend, wool, silk, or other natural materials, such as bamboo or corn. Make sure the batting you buy is at least six inches wider and six inches longer than your quilt top.

Accurate Cutting

Measuring and cutting accuracy are important for successful quilting. Measure at least twice, and cut once!

Cut strips across the fabric width unless directed otherwise.

Cutting for patchwork usually begins with cutting strips, which are then cut into smaller pieces. First, cut straight strips from a fat quarter:

1. Fold fat quarter in half with selvage edge at the top (*Photo A*).

2. Straighten edge of fabric by placing ruler atop fabric, aligning one of the lines on ruler with selvage edge of fabric (*Photo B*). Cut along right edge of ruler.

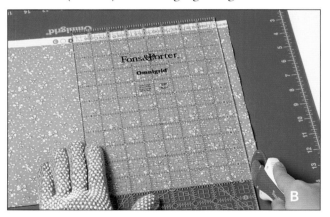

3. Rotate fabric, and use ruler to measure from cut edge to desired strip width (*Photo C*). Measurements in instructions include ¼" seam allowances.

4. After cutting the required number of strips, cut strips into squares and label them.

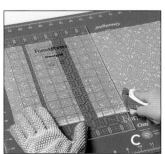

Setting up Your Sewing Machine

Sew Accurate ¼" Seams

Standard seam width for patchwork and quiltmaking is ¼". Some machines come with a patchwork presser foot, also known as a quarter-inch foot. If your machine doesn't have a quarter-inch foot, you may be able to purchase one from a dealer. Or, you can create a quarter-inch seam guide on your machine using masking tape or painter's tape.

Place an acrylic ruler on your sewing machine bed under the presser foot. Slowly turn handwheel until the tip of the needle barely rests atop the ruler's quarter-inch mark (*Photo A*). Make sure the lines on the ruler are parallel to the lines on the machine throat plate. Place tape on the machine bed along edge of ruler (*Photo B*).

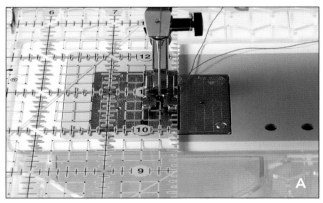

Take a Simple Seam Test

Seam accuracy is critical to machine piecing, so take this simple test once you have your quarter-inch presser foot on your machine or have created a tape guide.

Place 2 (2½") squares right sides together, and sew with a scant ¼" seam. Open squares and finger press seam. To finger press, with right sides facing you, press the seam to one side with your fingernail. Measure across pieces, raw edge to raw edge (*Photo C*). If they measure 4½", you have passed the test! Repeat the test as needed to make sure you can confidently sew a perfect ¼" seam.

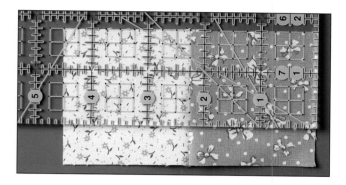

Sewing Comfortably

Other elements that promote pleasant sewing are good lighting, a comfortable chair, background music—and chocolate! Good lighting promotes accurate sewing. The better you can see what you are working on, the better your results. A comfortable chair enables you to sew for longer periods of time. An office chair with a good back rest and adjustable height works well. Music helps keep you relaxed. Chocolate is, for many quilters, simply a necessity.

Tips for Patchwork and Pressing

As you sew more patchwork, you'll develop your own shortcuts and favorite methods. Here are a few favored by many quilters:

● As you join patchwork units to form rows, and join rows to form blocks, press seams in opposite directions from row to row whenever possible (*Photo A*). By pressing seams one direction in the first row and the opposite direction in the next row, you will often create seam allowances that abut when rows are joined (*Photo B*). Abutting or nesting seams are ideal for forming perfectly matched corners on the right side of your quilt blocks and quilt top. Such pressing is not always possible, so don't worry if you end up with seam allowances facing the same direction as you join units.

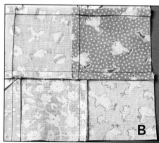

● Sew on and off a small, folded fabric square to prevent bobbin thread from bunching at throat plate (*Photo C*). You'll also save thread, which means fewer stops to wind bobbins, and fewer hanging threads to be snipped. Repeated use of the small piece of fabric gives it lots of thread "legs," so some quilters call it a spider.

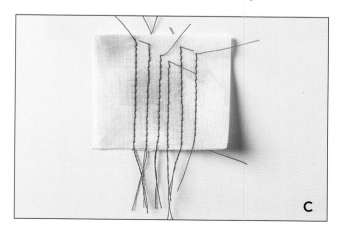

● Chain piece patchwork to reduce the amount of thread you use, and minimize the number and length of threads you need to trim from patchwork. Without cutting threads at the end of a seam, take 3–4 stitches without any fabric under the needle, creating a short thread chain approximately ⅛" long (*Photo D*). Repeat until you have a long line of pieces. Remove chain from machine, clip threads between units, and press seams.

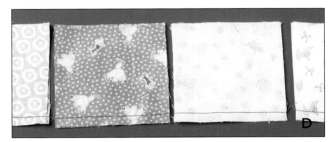

D

● Trim off tiny triangle tips (sometimes called dog ears) created when making triangle-square units (*Photo E*). Trimming triangles reduces bulk and makes patchwork units and blocks lie flatter. Though no one will see the back of your quilt top once it's quilted, a neat back free of dangling threads and patchwork points is the mark of a good quilter. Also, a smooth, flat quilt top is easier to quilt, whether by hand or machine.

E

● Careful pressing will make your patchwork neat and crisp, and will help make your finished quilt top lie flat. Ironing and pressing are two different skills. Iron fabric to remove wrinkles using a back and forth, smoothing motion. Press patchwork and quilt blocks by raising and gently lowering the iron atop your work. After sewing a patchwork unit, first press the seam with the unit closed, pressing to set, or embed, the stitching. Setting the seam this way will help produce straight, crisp seams. Open the unit and press on the right side with the seam toward the darkest

fabric, being careful to not form a pleat in your seam, and carefully pressing the patchwork flat.

● Many quilters use finger pressing to open and flatten seams of small units before pressing with an iron. To finger press, open patchwork unit with right side of fabric facing you. Run your fingernail firmly along seam, making sure unit is fully open with no pleat.

● Careful use of steam in your iron will make seams and blocks crisp and flat (*Photo F*). Aggressive ironing can stretch blocks out of shape, and is a common pitfall for new quilters.

F

Adding Borders

Follow these simple instructions to make borders that fit perfectly on your quilt.

1. Find the length of your quilt by measuring through the quilt center, not along the edges, since the edges may have stretched. Take 3 measurements and average them to determine the length to cut your side borders (*Diagram A*). Cut 2 side borders this length.

2. Fold border strips in half to find center. Pinch to create crease mark or place a pin at center. Fold quilt top in half crosswise to find center of side. Attach side borders to quilt center by pinning them at the ends and the center, and easing in any fullness. If quilt edge is a bit longer than border, pin and sew with border on top; if border is

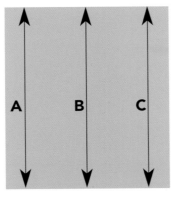

Diagram A

A —————

B —————

C —————

TOTAL —————

————— ÷3

AVERAGE
LENGTH —————

HELPFUL TIP
**Use the following decimal conversions to calculate
your quilt's measurements:**

⅛" = .125	⅝" = .625
¼" = .25	¾" = .75
⅜" = .375	⅞" = .875
½" = .5	

slightly longer than quilt top, pin and sew with border on the bottom. Machine feed dogs will ease in the fullness of the longer piece. Press seams toward borders.

3. Find the width of your quilt by measuring across the quilt and side borders (*Diagram B*). Take 3 measurements and average them to determine the length to cut your top and bottom borders. Cut 2 borders this length.

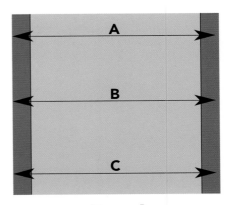

Diagram B

4. Mark centers of borders and top and bottom edges of quilt top. Attach top and bottom borders to quilt, pinning at ends and center, and easing in any fullness (*Diagram C*). Press seams toward borders.

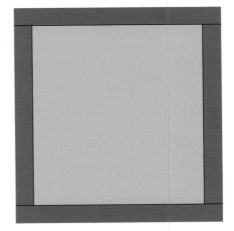

Diagram C

5. Gently steam press entire quilt top on one side and then the other. When pressing on wrong side, trim off any loose threads.

Joining Border Strips

Not all quilts have borders, but they are a nice complement to a quilt top. If your border is longer than 40", you will need to join 2 or more strips to make a border the required length. You can join border strips with either a straight seam parallel to the ends of the strips (*Photo A* on page 138), or with a diagonal seam. For the diagonal seam method, place one border strip perpendicular to another strip, rights sides facing (*Photo B*). Stitch diagonally across strips as shown. Trim seam allowance to ¼". Press seam open (*Photo C*).

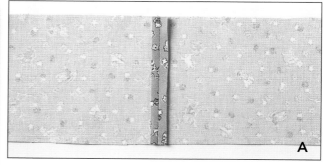

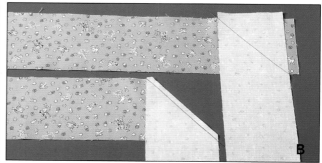

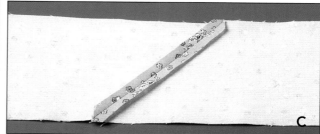

Quilting Your Quilt

Quilters today joke that there are three ways to quilt a quilt—by hand, by machine, or by check. Some enjoy making quilt tops so much, they prefer to hire a professional machine quilter to finish their work. The Split Nine Patch baby quilt shown at left has simple machine quilting that you can do yourself.

Decide what color thread will look best on your quilt top before choosing your backing fabric. A thread color that will blend in with the quilt top is a good choice for beginners. Choose backing fabric that will blend with your thread as well. A print fabric is a good choice for hiding less-than-perfect machine quilting. The backing fabric must be at least 3"–4" larger than your quilt top on all 4 sides. For example: if your quilt top measures 44" × 44", your backing needs to be at least 50" × 50". If your quilt top is 80" × 96", then your backing fabric needs to be at least 86" × 102".

For quilt tops 36" wide or less, use a single width of fabric for the backing. Buy enough length to allow adequate margin at quilt edges, as noted above. When your quilt is wider than 36", one option is to use 60"-, 90"-, or 108"-wide fabric for the quilt backing. Because fabric selection is limited for wide fabrics, quilters generally piece the quilt backing from 44/45"-wide fabric. Plan on 40"–42" of usable fabric width when estimating how much fabric to purchase. Plan your piecing strategy to avoid having a seam along the vertical or horizontal center of the quilt.

For a quilt 37"–60" wide, a backing with horizontal seams is usually the most economical use of fabric. For example, for a quilt 50" × 70", vertical seams would require 152", or 4¼ yards, of 44/45"-wide fabric (76" + 76" = 152"). Horizontal seams would require 112", or 3¼ yards (56" + 56" = 112").

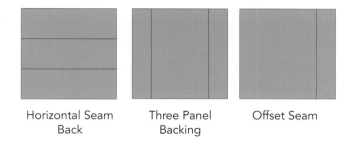

Horizontal Seam Back   Three Panel Backing   Offset Seam

For a quilt 61"–80" wide, most quilters piece a three-panel backing, with vertical seams, from two lengths of fabric. Cut one of the pieces in half lengthwise, and sew the halves to opposite sides of the wider panel. Press the seams away from the center panel.

For a quilt 81"–120" wide, you will need three lengths of fabric, plus extra margin. For example, for a quilt 108" × 108", purchase at least 342", or 9½ yards, of 44/45"-wide fabric (114" + 114" + 114" = 342").

For a three-panel backing, pin the selvage edge of the center panel to the selvage edge of the side panel, with edges aligned and right sides facing. Machine stitch with a ½" seam. Trim seam allowances to ¼", trimming off the selvages from both panels at once. Press the seam away from the center of the quilt. Repeat on other side of center panel.

For a two-panel backing, join panels in the same manner as above, and press the seam to one side.

Create a "quilt sandwich" by layering your backing, batting, and quilt top. Find the crosswise center of the backing fabric by folding it in half. Mark with a pin on each side. Lay backing down on a table or floor, wrong side up. Tape corners and edges of backing to the surface with masking or painter's tape so that backing is taut (*Photo A*).

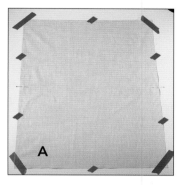

Fold batting in half crosswise and position it atop backing fabric, centering folded edge at center of backing (*Photo B*). Unfold batting and smooth it out atop backing (*Photo C*).

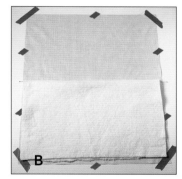 

In the same manner, fold the quilt top in half crosswise and center it atop backing and batting (*Photo D*). Unfold top and smooth it out atop batting (*Photo E*).

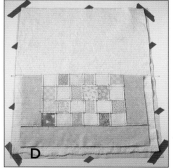 

Use safety pins to pin baste the layers (*Photo F*). Pins should be about a fist width apart. A special tool, called a Kwik Klip, or a grapefruit spoon makes closing the pins easier. As you slide a pin through all three layers, slide the point of the pin into one of the tool's grooves. Push on the tool to help close the pin.

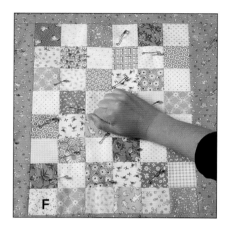

For straight line quilting, install an even feed or walking foot on your machine. This presser foot helps all three layers of your quilt move through the machine evenly without bunching.

Walking Foot

Stitching "in the ditch"

An easy way to quilt your first quilt is to stitch "in the ditch" along seam lines. No marking is needed for this type of quilting.

Binding Your Quilt

Preparing Binding

Strips for quilt binding may be cut either on the straight of grain or on the bias.

1. Measure the perimeter of your quilt and add approximately 24" to allow for mitered corners and finished ends.
2. Cut the number of strips necessary to achieve desired length. We like to cut binding strips 2¼" wide.
3. Join your strips with diagonal seams into 1 continuous piece (*Photo A*). Press the seams open. (See page 142 for instructions for the diagonal seams method of joining strips.)

4. Press your binding in half lengthwise, with wrong sides facing, to make French-fold binding (*Photo B*).

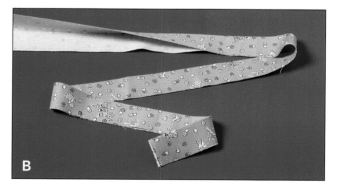

Attaching Binding

Attach the binding to your quilt using an even-feed or walking foot. This prevents puckering when sewing through the three layers.

1. Choose beginning point along one side of quilt. Do not start at a corner. Match the two raw edges of the binding strip to the raw edge of the quilt top. The folded edge

will be free and to left of seam line (*Photo C*). Leave 12" or longer tail of binding strip dangling free from beginning point. Stitch, using ¼" seam, through all layers.

Bring binding straight down in line with next edge to be sewn, leaving top fold even with raw edge of previously sewn side (*Photo F*). Begin stitching at top edge, sewing through all layers (*Photo G*).

2. For mitered corners, stop stitching ¼" from corner; backstitch, and remove quilt from sewing machine (*Photo D*). Place a pin ¼" from corner to mark where you will stop stitching.

Rotate quilt quarter turn and fold binding straight up, away from corner, forming 45-degree-angle fold (*Photo E*).

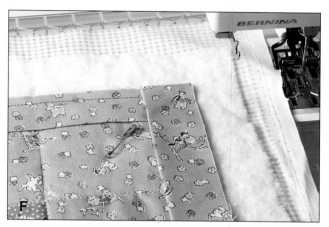

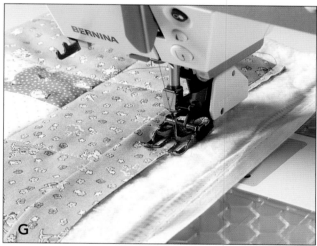

3. To finish binding, stop stitching about 8" away from starting point, leaving about a 12" tail at end (*Photo H*). Bring beginning and end of binding to center of 8" opening and fold each back, leaving about ¼" space

between the two folds of binding (*Photo I*). (Allowing this ¼" extra space is critical, as binding tends to stretch when it is stitched to the quilt. If the folded ends meet at this point, your binding will be too long for the space after the ends are joined.) Crease folds of binding with your fingernail.

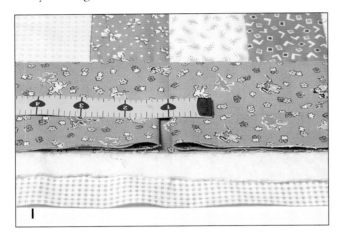

4. Open out each edge of binding and draw line across wrong side of binding on creased fold line, as shown in *Photo J*. Draw line along lengthwise fold of binding at same spot to create an X (*Photo K*).

5. With edge of ruler at marked X, line up 45-degree-angle marking on ruler with one long side of binding (*Photo L*). Draw diagonal line across binding as shown in *Photo M*.

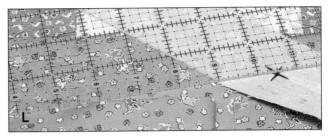

Repeat for other end of binding. Lines must angle in same direction (*Photo N*).

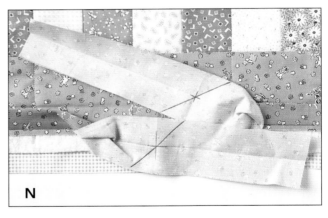

6. Pin binding ends together with right sides facing, pin-matching diagonal lines as shown in *Photo O*. Binding ends will be at right angles to each other. Machine-stitch along diagonal line, removing pins as you stitch (*Photo P*).

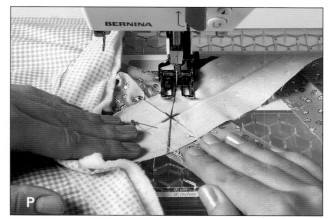

7. Lay binding against quilt to double-check that it is correct length (*Photo Q*). Trim ends of binding ¼" from diagonal seam (*Photo R*).

8. Finger press diagonal seam open (*Photo S*). Fold binding in half and finish stitching binding to quilt (*Photo T*).

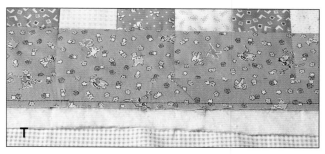

Hand Stitching Binding to Quilt Back

1. Trim any excess batting and quilt back with scissors or a rotary cutter (*Photo A*). Leave enough batting (about ⅛" beyond quilt top) to fill binding uniformly when it is turned to quilt back.

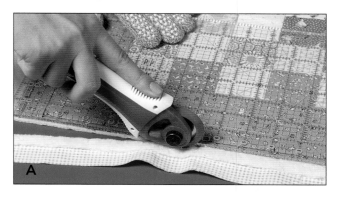

2. Bring folded edge of binding to quilt back so that it covers machine stitching. Blindstitch folded edge to quilt backing, using a few pins just ahead of stitching to hold binding in place (*Photo B*).

3. Continue stitching to corner. Fold unstitched binding from next side under, forming a 45-degree angle and a mitered corner. Stitch mitered folds on both front and back (*Photo C*).

Finishing Touches

● **Label your quilt so the recipient and future generations know who made it.** To make a label, use a fabric marking pen to write the details on a small piece of solid color fabric (*Photo A*). To make writing easier, put pieces of masking tape on the wrong side. Remove tape after writing. Use your iron to turn under ¼" on each edge, then stitch the label to the back of your quilt using a blindstitch, taking care not to sew through to quilt top.

● **Take a photo of your quilt.** Keep your photos in an album or journal along with notes, fabric swatches, and other information about the quilts.

● **If your quilt is a gift, include care instructions.** Some quilt shops carry pre-printed care labels you can sew onto the quilt (*Photo B*). Or, make a care label using the method described above.

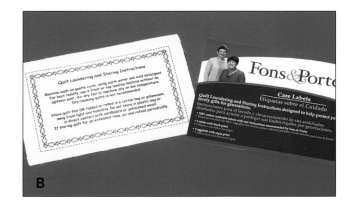